The Green Hedge Witch

The Green Hedge Witch

A Guide to Wild Magic

RAE BETH

Illustrated by Jan Nesbitt

ROBERT HALE · LONDON

© Rae Beth 2008
First published in Great Britain 2008

ISBN 978 0 7090 8585 0

Robert Hale Limited
Clerkenwell House
Clerkenwell Green
London EC1R 0HT

www.halebooks.com

The right of Rae Beth to be identified as author of this
work has been asserted by her in accordance
with the Copyright, Designs and Patents Act 1988

A catalogue record for this book is available from the British Library

2   4   6   8   10   9   7   5   3

Typeset by Derek Doyle and Associates, Shaw Heath
Printed and bound by the MPG Books Group, Bodmin and King's Lynn

This is dedicated to my children,
Emily LeQuesne and Liam Austin

CONTENTS

Acknowledgements

The people who have helped to make this book appear are really too numerous to mention, but I'd like especially to thank: John Hale, Helen and Harry Knibb, Jan Nesbitt, Alan and Pauline Royce of Glastonbury and, last but not least, my husband and magical partner, Ashley Pascoe.

Chapter 1

Crossing the Boundaries

I am a caster of spells using natural magic and I do healing work with the elves. This is a book for budding spell-casters – and for experienced workers as well – about some ways we can each help and heal at this time of environmental crisis – a subject about which elves are passionate! Some of the methods described are quite complex. But if you are a complete beginner you can make powerful magic with elves straightaway by choosing the more simple techniques from amongst what follows and applying them in the ways that suit you best. (It is not always the most technically knowledgeable who are most effective. Rather, it is those whose work is heartfelt.)

'Help heal the natural world?' I hear some people say. 'Isn't that rather presumptuous? Isn't it people and their attitudes that really need healing? And what can little hedge witches do?

It is true that Mother Earth doesn't need our help if she is to survive. She will do that, anyway. And I don't foresee doom and gloom for this world on a grand scale. Life will go on. But the writing *is* on the wall for the human relationship with the rest of the natural world. We cannot go on like this – chopping down rainforests, abusing Earth's resources, polluting land and sea. The biosphere will break down if we don't change our ways. And as a hedge witch who is leading a human life, I feel that I must take some responsibility. I must do what I can to help initiate a healing change, using my psychic and magical healing skills.

I am not alone. There are many who feel this way.

If the worst should come to the worst, the biosphere would repair anyway – eventually. Mother Earth is creative and innovative. Her spirit is life in evolution. There will be new plants and creatures, whatever happens. Since I believe in reincarnation, I also feel there will be many more lives here – future lives – for such as we, humans (and elves and all kinds of creatures) trying to learn how to live more wisely. However, I don't foresee the worst happening. In any case and whatever happens, we shall all survive as a part of the whole. After all, we are each a part of the same indestructible, infinite, multi-dimensional universe. Each of us, like the earth, the trees, the creatures, is made of stardust. The question is not *whether* we will be, but *what* we will be. And for how long? The same goes for plants, other creatures and places.

That particular tree you pass each day on your walk through town, will that be ruthlessly, pointlessly chopped down? Will your or my local forest survive for a while longer? Or will it be sacrificed to 'development'? Will skylarks become a thing of the past? Will New York, Rio de Janeiro, London, Amsterdam, Alexandria all drown, together with many other places? It's looking like a possibility, scientists tell us.

How big a spell would it take to save all we love in its present form? A spell with a big enough amount of love in it, that may be the answer. (And *many* people feel that much love for the natural world, as do the elves and all kinds of creatures. So I am – cautiously – optimistic.)

By ourselves, we can each only do our bit. And that is what this book is all about really, the spells and rites we *can* do regularly. And which might add up, in the end, collectively, to something that's rather big.

From every faith and culture all around the world, very many people are now casting healing spells, saying prayers, enacting rituals to try to help and heal nature and remake the human relationship with all the natural world. Perhaps you are already joining in or would like to do so. If that is the case, I hope you will find many useful ideas within this book. What you will not find is some kind of cult or a dogmatic religion. You can do this kind of magical healing work (or add some of it to what you already do) whatever else you do or do not believe.

There are two main themes in the following text. The first is the making of a good new relationship with elves – those spirit presences who dwell in or can be psychically contacted through nature. The elves are not actually nature spirits in the same way that the spirit of an animal species or a living tree (or a living human come to that) is such a thing. Instead, they are dwellers within what is called 'the Otherworld', an umbrella term for subtle parallel dimensions of the Earth. These beings, known usually as elves or faeries of various kinds, have had a long relationship with human beings. In the Pagan era they were welcomed and their blessing was often sought upon crops and livestock and human affairs. More recently, they have been shunned and feared and then, more recently still, ridiculed, belief in them relegated to 'matters for children'. But they are still there.

Sometimes, in folklore, they have been known for strong aggression towards humans who cut down trees wantonly or who block the faerie paths with buildings.

(These 'paths' may be what we know now as leys or ley-lines, Earth's bio-electrical meridians.) Elves and faeries dislike people who cause offence against nature. They are said, in some cases, to curse the offenders with much bad luck or to fire faerie arrows, known as 'elf-shot' which bring diseases.

Is this all real let alone moral? Our ancestors seem to have thought so. My own elven teachers, however, do not advocate the bringing down of curses or firing of elf-shot at anybody. Neither they nor I believe that it has any connection with any true healing. With warfare, yes, but I am no psychic warrior. And I certainly don't think the Earth needs another war – of any kind. However, the point remains that a cruel or unhealthy relationship with nature must result in ill-luck or disease in the end, for everyone. (We already live in a world that is gradually being stripped of natural beauty. Without trees to shade and shield us, our crops and our animals from too much sun and wind, and, above all, to be the frame and roof beam for the natural world, how healthy or fortunate can anyone really be?)

Looked at like that, the elves may be seen not only as real beings but also as symbols for some consequences of our actions. As such, they warn us of the perils of alien-ation from trees and creatures and all our kin throughout all of nature. On this basis, I hope that any reader who cannot believe in elves as actual objective beings, as real as cats or bears, will still be able to work with the magic I shall describe, perceiving it as a symbolic and psychic process for coming into a better alignment with nature and for bringing healing.

I myself believe in elves as real beings – more real than many of the humans portrayed in today's films. (Though that wouldn't be difficult. Hollywood-style humans are not convincing.)

I consider elves to be an actual species – or rather a collection of species – but of an otherworldly origin. By this, I do not mean that they are from Mars or another universe. Nor from some realm unconnected with nature. Rather, they are from subtle dimensions of nature, parallel with and affected by our own, as ours is also affected by them. Their otherworldliness is a metaphor to describe – from a human point of view – their less than tangible nature when they are in our realm. (They are perfectly substantial when in their own.)

This difference in tangibility has not always been so marked. There are plenty of folkloric accounts of people who married elves in the past and lived with them and had children, here in our world. Nevertheless, the faeries, the elves, have always been more ethereal than humans, and can have great trouble in coming to terms with the harshness and crudity of human culture.

Elves and faeries are from a different dimension from our own but it *is* of the Earth. All this is difficult to describe. The words I am using or could use here must bestride some kind of boundary between quantum physics and poetry. I can only say that, to me, the elven realm is real objectively.

The other theme within this book is that of hedge witchcraft, an old tradition. It is one that you may not perceive in the same way that I do – as a magnificent, deeply healing thing, potentially. Witches of all kinds in the past have also cursed (or blessed) other people. They have sometimes done so for money or their own advantage. (Unfortunately, any human practice at all can be degraded, including science, mainstream religion, hedge witchcraft and cookery. They are each only as wholesome – or as free from harm – as the people who practise them.) But this is not an academic treatise about hedge witchcraft and the people (of many kinds) who have practised it over the centuries. Instead, it is a look at what I believe to be the uncorrupted essence of this ancient magic. And at ideas for working with it in today's world.

Why witchcraft at all as a prime healing method? It has such a dubious reputation. And why hedge witchcraft, especially? (What is it? Something to do with herbs?) Read on and judge of all this for yourself. But I will just say that it is *because* witchcraft has been so feared and shunned that it has become an unacknowledged repository of some important concepts and techniques for magical healing. It is like an old trunk full of dust and cobwebs and bits of dead toad and things written in blood. And amongst all of this there are magical tools of incredible beauty, and teachings from elves, and ways of bringing healing change that are not found elsewhere – or not very often.

Hedge witchcraft works on and across the boundary between our everyday reality and the domain of wild spirit presences. You do not, however, have to work literally within a hedgerow to do it. Forest edges, beaches, hilltops and other liminal places will do as well. You can even practise indoors, creating a meeting place between the mundane and the magical within your home.

As I said, hedge witchcraft is very old. It is a form of natural magic done by a witch when on their own (with regard to other human beings) rather than in any group or coven. In other words, it is the work done by the traditional wise woman or cunning man. Today, it is often aligned with Wicca, the modern nature-based spirituality blending Pagan celebrations with spell-casting. But the oldest hedge witchcraft has some traits which are all its own.

Hedge witchcraft works upon and with relationships between humanity and the land, and between this tangible

Earth and the elven realms. That is its domain. It is this work, private and (usually, nowadays) entirely unacknowledged by human society, that makes hedge witchcraft such a profound practice. Traditionally, we hedge witches have aimed to bring balance between what is 'beyond the hedge', the realm of wild nature spirits, elves and all creatures, and what is 'within the hedge', the human community. Now, more than ever, a healing balance needs to be struck between human needs and those of the natural world. No wonder the spirits who guard the tradition of hedge witchcraft are keen to revive it. (And they are telling me – psychically – that they are keen.)

Foremost amongst those beings who have been perceived as beyond the hedge are faeries of all kinds. Do not be misled by this word 'faerie'. The type that I work with most, known as elves, can be implacable representatives of Earth's more subtle and magical dimensions and formidable experts on such tricky and complex matters as natural law and natural justice. Many are of human size or larger. They are a witch's allies in work of magical healing that serves *their* interests, which is to say that helps nature and restores natural balance and joyfulness.

Harmony between humanity and the Earth's 'unearthly' spirit presences is the hedge witch's concern. But we do also cast love spells, make charms for prosperity and so on – all the expected stock-in-trade of the witch. We do these things from the particular stance of the hedge witch. That is to say, with one foot in the everyday world and the other in faerie, the realm of untamed spirits. To do this, you must be on a boundary between two places, somewhere that partakes of each of them, such as a hedge.

The word 'liminal' means 'threshold' and is applied to areas where we can step out of one place (or state of consciousness, since it is a psychological term) and into another. These thresholds are places of psychic transition. They can also be fairly described as being 'between the worlds'. They are between realms physically and also, for those who know suitable magical techniques, psychically. Among such places are beaches (which are between land and sea), hilltops (between the land and sky), edges of woodland or forest (between open country or agricultural land and wild woodland) and hedgerows or even fences (between a settlement, farm, garden or park and what is beyond it. Or between subdivisions of these, such as one field and another).

There are some old words from the Northern European Pagan tradition which show the derivation of the term 'hedge witch'. One is the German word *hagazissa*, which means 'hedge sitter'. It shares a linguistic root with the modern German *hexe* meaning 'witch' and the English 'hex'. In his book *Helrunar*, the writer Jan Fries tells us that the *hagazissa* was a person who could go between the world of the human settlement and that of wild spirits, elves and ghosts, who were beyond the psychic limits around the village. Thus, symbolically, they straddled the hedge which protected the human community and could relate to those on each side of it. This dual consciousness – almost, we might say, dual nationality – gave them magical powers and allies or, as we should now say, familiar spirits. The name *hagazissa* was applied to both women and men, as is the present-day term 'hedge witch'.

Another relevant word, mentioned by Michael Howard in his book *Mysteries of the Runes*, is *haegtessa*. This means 'hedge rider' and is a Saxon term for night-flying witches.

As I said, these words *hagazissa* and *haegtessa* do contain or share the linguistic origins of hedge witchcraft. But I'd like to make two things clear. One is that the practice was not confined to Germany, nor even to Germanic people who entered and lived in other lands, such as Britain. The art of changing our consciousness at will by sitting out at a liminal place, the better to practise magic, was known throughout Northern Europe, including those areas which we call Celtic. Furthermore, the same practice (in many forms and not necessarily involving hedgerows) has been known throughout the world, in very many indigenous cultures. That is because it does work.

My second point is that hedge witchcraft is an adaptable, evolving practice. That means we do not have to do it exactly as we think our ancestors did it but in a style that suits us now, in our present culture. And actually, I would bet my best dress and half my queendom that our ancestors did not do their hedge witchcraft exactly as their own ancestors had. That is because anything that is alive and not a museum piece evolves and changes with changing times.

I do not mean to imply by this that tradition isn't important. It is vital. It is the source upon which we draw for our renewed inspiration. There is a wealth of old knowledge upon which we can base today's hedge witchcraft. Some is in what we know of the Pagan practices of our ancestors and some in folklore. Some has been hidden in faerie tales and some recorded by nineteenth-century collectors of folk beliefs and some passed on by word of mouth down the generations.

But the hedge witch has probably always been inclined to put their own twist on tradition and to be adventurous. We have certainly always been influenced by the prevailing trends in the wider world. For example, when the Christian Church was at the height of its political and cultural powers, many of us incorporated Christian prayers and the invocation of Christian saints into our Pagan natural magic. I'd say we're explorers and adapters and that we do not enjoy cultural rigidity even though we are custodians of some very old knowledge.

In ancient times, even as long ago as the Neolithic era, human communities were protected by thick thorn hedges. These barriers helped to keep people and livestock safe from robbers and wild animals. But a people who could not venture beyond their protective boundary could become imprisoned by it. They were cut off from adventure and from any good new ideas which those from outside could have brought and from the tonic effect of untamed nature. Someone was needed to strike a good psychic balance between 'civilization' and 'nature'. And that job fell to the hedge sitter. Our task was to merge and balance these polarities within our selves, on behalf of the village. Having done so we could and can cast many spells for healing purposes and speak with spirits.

These practices stem from a change of consciousness, a deeper, stronger psychic awareness (achieved by a suitable spell for the purpose) and by the making of friends in elven realms. Sitting by a hedge or beneath a tree in a field corner or at the edge of a woodland – or even amongst house plants in our own home – is a great help to us. Obviously, it does not automatically lead to having a conversation with spirits or casting a spell but it is a key factor.

The psychic atmosphere of trees is connected with the deep dreaming nature of each tree spirit. Also, the sound of the wind among branches and leaves is lightly hypnotic. If you apply but a small effort to turn your attention towards spirit realms while among trees you can find the veils between yourself and a psychic reality part very easily. (The main reason why this does not *always* happen is that we have been taught by mainstream culture to ignore or mistrust the signs.)

'Sitting out', whether in a hedgerow or not, was an old custom amongst tribal workers of magic. In Northern Europe, its name was the *utiseta*. This meant going somewhere away from your tribe or village's routine existence to spend time alone in a sacred place speaking with spirits. If you wished to consult your ancestors, the chosen spot would be a burial mound. If the idea was to speak with the faeries, a known resort of theirs would be chosen instead. This might be a hill-top or forest glade where they were known to appear and dance. (Britain has many such faerie-haunted spots mentioned in folklore.)

As with the Native American 'vision quest' or, come to that, any pilgrimage, it was the fact of journeying that did very much to open a person's mind to the presence of spirits. All that you really needed to do when you got there was call to the elves – or ancestors or nature spir-its – out loud or in your mind and place offerings to them upon the ground. These would be gifts like honey, mead, cream, cakes, garlands of flowers, precious stones. Good things and treasures. Nowadays we do the same. But it is correct to bury the gifts, disturbing the land and its local flora as little as possible in the process. This is a magical act conveying the offerings into the spirit world. Needless to say, as hedge witches, we offer only natural things or objects which are biodegradable.

Simply being amongst trees and other plants is a psychic boost. Today however we usually need to add spells to the practice of 'sitting' to get good results and I will explain these, as well as more complex outdoor rites, in later chapters.

The very first time I saw one of the light-elves here, in this earthly realm where we live out our daily lives (and not while in some kind of trance but wide awake in my everyday consciousness) I was walking alone in a wood. I was about seventeen at the time so this was in the 1960s, an era when the English countryside was very quiet and peaceful so it was easy to be alone and undis-turbed in a wood. But when I say 'alone', I mean with respect to human beings. To anyone who has the nature or temperament of a hedge sitter, the woods are thronged with others – tree spirits, birds, all manner of wild creatures, elemental spirits of wind, light, water, land and wraith (ghost substance), elves of all kinds . . . We don't always see them but we can sense them. Anyway, this wood, called Thickwood (at the southern end of the Cotswolds) is quite big for south-west England. To someone from Germany, Poland, Finland, Brazil or anywhere really forested, it would be just a tiny copse. However, my experience just goes to show that the presence of quite a small number of trees can make an environment in which wild spirit encounters are simple, easy.

On this day, I had a particularly fierce hunger for faerie realms. I was not an especially naïve teenager and probably much more interested in sex, alcohol and breaking the adult rules of conventionality than were a great many of my contemporaries. I pursued all the above with relish. (I make this point to show that meetings with those from the Otherworld can't always be dismissed as fantasy born of repressions and inhibitions.) Anyway, I believed that there was no reason why I should not meet with an elf, since I already felt that the faerie Otherworld and its values meant 'home' to me.

I walked along quietly, reaching out in my mind, projecting my thoughts towards my image of elven territory, which was of a forest like Thickwood but wilder, larger and somehow more real – as though this world that we live in were of mist and shadows and faerie more actual. I called out and asked if one of them would be so kind as to meet me here, as a favour. After a while, my efforts were rewarded. A silvery-blue figure appeared in front of me. I stopped and stared. He was about my own height and clad in trousers and a tunic. I was so pleased to have had my request granted that I was just struck dumb with relief. And then I managed to stutter, 'Thank you, this is wonderful' and things like 'This means so much to me' till the elf disappeared. He must have thought 'What a strange young woman. Not much of a conversationalist.' And he may have also felt compassion for one so unaware (at the time) of her own magical abilities and real nature.

The world has grown much noisier, psychically as well as physically, since I was seventeen. But a hedge witch can still meet with elves. In Britain, they are often around, especially on the seashore or amongst trees. If you are naturally psychic you may see them quite easily once you start looking for them. Often, I think it is a matter of giving ourselves permission to see them since this is against the rules of what mainstream culture calls being in touch with the 'real world'.

If we talk to the elves, they do hear us. After all, the 'Otherworld' is not completely somewhere else. It is, in today's terminology, a parallel dimension, a subtle aspect of this world, here. I'll say that again. It is another aspect of our own world. It is not super-natural but within nature. In my opinion, there is nothing outside nature. There is just Nature, vaster more mysterious and magical than most people ever dream. Nowadays, saying this sort of thing is rather like Galileo telling the Church that the Earth goes around the sun. (But all the same, it does.)

If we talk to the elves (or to nature spirits or anything that we might term a 'spirit presence') they hear us in their minds. It is, so they tell me, as though someone whispered in their ear. Whether or not they respond depends partly on what they think of our sincerity and possible motives. Any answer from spirit realms should be taken seriously and not dismissed as 'a trick of the light' or 'your mind playing tricks'. It is true that illusions appear (and the faeries are notorious for creating illusion and trickery if they should feel like enjoying a joke at human expense) but if we do not keep our minds open then we can miss the real thing.

Real encounters have an unforced quality which is unmistakable. All that we need to do to have such experiences is to enter a state of consciousness in which we accept them. Believe it or not, this can be achieved by simply going for a walk or 'sitting out' in a green leafy place. It is such a basic human impulse, this idea of going for a walk 'outside', beyond the hedge or forest edge, away from other people and social activity. And it can introduce us to the basics of hedge witchcraft.

As I said earlier, the hedge sitter was well recognized in old Germany, and was a person with an important role. But the same or similar techniques were probably in use everywhere. There is even a hint of something similar in ancient Egypt. There has been and still is an Egyptian practice called 'Zar' which consists of working with spirits for magical healing. Zar practitioners contact the spirits mainly by singing and this is accompanied by rhythmic swaying of the body. Unlike hedge witchcraft however, which is a solitary practice, its devotees work together in groups. Zar is said to have been founded by a healer from upper Egypt called Zara. Her name apparently derives from A Gama which means 'a hedge, a thicket'. (I do not know if they had hedges in ancient Egypt. I certainly can't picture one near the pyramids. But I am sure they had thickets and still do.)

Is it just coincidence, this connection with a hedge or thicket in Zara's name? Or was there spirit work, hedge witchcraft based upon sitting out and all the magic of trees, herbs and elven presences, in ancient Egypt? I don't see why not. The present Zar cult is not like that, as I said, so it's all a bit vague, this surmise of mine. But it is possible. I am not trying to claim that hedge witchcraft began in

Egypt, any more than in Northern Europe, just that it or something like it may have been practised throughout the world. When something works, it tends to be discovered – with regional variations – everywhere.

Chapter 2

ꞕedge Witchcraft and the World Wood

Hedges are made up of trees and trees are, ultimately, the essence of forest. But there is really only one forest in all the world. We can call this the World Wood because it is made up of all the trees and shrubs in all parts of the globe, throughout the ages. The trees in our gardens are part of it. So are the hedges round them and round any field, the trees in our local park or on any roadside and all the trees surrounded by concrete in carparks. Each of the little copses and woodlands in Britain are in the World Wood. The enormous forests in Poland, Germany and Scandinavia are very large pieces of it. The rainforests of South America and on other continents too are the largest of all.

The World Wood is also comprised of all the trees that have ever lived, including those in primeval forests where dinosaurs walked. *And* it includes all trees that will *ever* be in times to come, their spirit presences, ghosts of the future.

Throughout time the World Wood shifts shape and area, growing strong here and dwindling there, growing back as the Ice Ages recede. And it evolves. The gigantic ferns of the earliest Earth forests became the birch, rowan and willow and all the multitudes of other species in present-day woodland. Who knows what is to come next?

So when we sit beside some shrub in a garden or field

corner or in a small copse, we can remember this. Any tree connects us with ancient forests where birds sang so loudly at dawn we should have needed earplugs to sleep through it. (But who would have wanted to?) This would have been the case in Britain not too long ago – a wild orchestra of birdsong from coast to coast.

Within the World Wood are all the medicines anyone can ever need. In fact, it is believed that many are as yet undiscovered by humans and may remain so, becoming extinct before we can learn of them. Here are all the herbs that can heal or destroy. Here also are the means of enchantment, the wands and the words by which we cast spells, the words we speak. Trees create air we can breathe by taking in carbon dioxide through their leaves and giving out oxygen. They make the world's atmosphere. Without them, there would be no breath for spell-casting words, no wind to carry them, no music, no birds.

See any tree and we see an example of Mother Earth's very own wands and staffs, standing upright in the land and casting the spell of creating an atmosphere in which all life can be. This seems to me something to emulate in our own magical work: the production of life-sustaining air and a good psychic atmosphere.

It is well known that faeries, witches and wizards use wands and staffs for casting spells. But it is rarely remembered that we can do this most powerfully by aligning ourselves with the magic of the World Wood. It is the vitality of this Great Forest that is assisting us each time we wield a wand. Hedge witchcraft is but one name for this alliance. It is a green magic and can restore harmony and help to create a healthier world, at least potentially. We can each wield this power more easily to the extent that we can allow ourselves to be at one – in spirit – with the World Wood. For we are not controllers of the Wood, we hedge witches. We do not own the Great Forest and its deep magic. In fact, it actually owns us and all other beings. Our real power begins when we can acknowledge that. The techniques of a hedge witch can help us achieve such an acknowledgement – as an ecstatic experience – and also to act upon it.

Around and within the World Wood there flows the water of the World Ocean, which is made up of all seas on Earth. And the World Wood exists in the ocean, too, as the 'hedge' of kelp, bladderwrack and other seaweeds that grow along the coast. This 'hedge of the sea' helps to mark the liminal place where land meets water. It is a powerful area for hedge witchcraft and one of my favourites. (Not all our hedges are in really obvious places and they are widespread.)

Furthermore, this World Wood weaves all the basic elements of life together. These, as understood by most present-day workers of magic, are air, fire, water, earth and wraith. The term 'wraith' as applied to the fifth element is not a common one although I like it. More widely known are the terms chi, prana, ond, aether/ether or spirit. Each of them refers to subtle and only semi-physical energy which is regarded as the most powerful as well as most refined of the elements. It is also by far the most mysterious, being, as witches say, 'everywhere and nowhere'.

Trees, as we know, help to create the very atmosphere needed to sustain Earth life and they cleanse air of many pollutants. Their leaves (and those of all other plants) convert the fire of sunlight, by photosynthesis, into the living green of the world's vegetation. Water, which is evaporated from the sea by the fire of the sun, is often precipitated as rain when clouds meet forested land. This water is then held in the land by roots and fallen leaves, having been shielded from evaporation by greenery. It sinks deep, to rise up again in the form of springs which become lakes or streams and rivers. In the element of earth, which is partly nourished by leaf mould, flourish the many, many creatures who crawl, slither, or walk within the World Wood, including ourselves. The spirit energy of trees (their chi, prana, ond, wraith or aether) is so incredibly mighty and generous that it sustains and feeds the vitality of anyone who goes near it. (That is one reason why walking in woodlands is such a tonic.) Besides, the World Wood contains spirit presences of many kinds: elves and white hinds, black dogs, faerie woodpeckers, green jacks and green knights, ghostly outlaws and the occasional wraith of a horseman or horsewoman, still 'steadily cantering through' on any number of ancient tracks that used to run through the forest and no longer do so – or not physically.

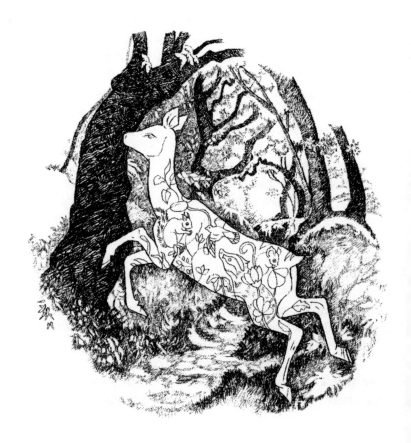

Clearly, the five basic elements of all life, air, fire, water, earth and spirit, are swirled into every life form by the great wand power of the World Wood. We all depend on it. Therefore, when we are psychically aligned with trees, in a spirit of co-operation for mutual benefit, our wands and staffs, broomsticks and potions are much more effective. Magic is easier and more joyful because the lone hedge witch is thus supported by and joined with many other spirit presences within the World Wood. Not really alone, at all. This approach is the very opposite of the exploitative one held within mainstream culture today. We don't use or command the trees or the tree spirits residing in wands or staffs. Instead, we form alliances with them.

These alliances can be cultivated by many psychic exercises and magical rites. One of my favourites is the simple practice of blessing a species and then breathing in the healing essence of that kind of tree, while acknowledging an interdependence. This can be done daily as a way of being in a healthy 'give and take' relationship with trees, on a magical basis. In the form which I shall describe, it brings psychic purification and enhances general levels of well-being and vitality.

Tree Breathing

Go for a walk and find a tree in a peaceful place. You can make do with visualizing this if you are far from trees or from peaceful places. Or you can work with a houseplant indoors. Take with you some fresh spring water or milk or beer.

An ideal choice of tree for the following spell would be a birch but you may also work with any non-poisonous species. And here I must comment that anyone practising natural magic must learn to identify trees and other plants before working with them. Those who can't tell a yew tree from a beech or a buddleia from a laburnum may be in some danger. To breathe the pollen of some trees may cause some illness if you are frail or if you have an allergic response. In summer when leaves are on all the trees it is quite easy to tell them apart with the help of an illustrated guide (such as from the Collins Gem series).

If you are working in your garden and concentrating on psychic purification and vitality or health, you might choose for your ally a bush of sage, rosemary or lavender.

Indoors, you might work with a houseplant of non-poisonous species. These green familiar spirits can be very good to us. An ideal choice might be a peace lily, a rubber plant or an English ivy.

Plants that live indoors in Europe are often at home in rainforests. (So if you live in Brazil or any other such tropical area, you may be able to work with them outside.) Such houseplants and others are good at cleaning the atmosphere. They transmute formaldehydes, ammonia and other toxins present in soft furnishings and cleaning fluids. If we approach the spirits of such plants to ask for help, they will do just as good a job for us psychically.

But as hedge sitters, witches who mediate between humans and the rest of the natural world, we must give to the plants – magically – as well as taking help from them. We can do this by beginning with a blessing for them.

Walk all around the tree. Touch it and greet it, aloud or in your mind. Take the time to feel the psychic atmosphere of the tree. Then, resting one hand upon a branch or a leaf, say this.

Spell of Blessing and of Being Blessed

In the names of Mother Earth
and the Green God of Trees,
may you be blessed, tree of [name the species]
with health and increase,
you and all your kind,
in harmony with all other species.
By all the powers of wind, light, rain, land and wraith,
so may this be.

Then add, 'I bring you a gift.'

Pour out the water or milk or beer from your bottle at the foot of the tree. Say, 'Blessed be. And I ask that you bless me.'

Stand and breathe in quite slowly and deeply of the tree's atmosphere. Say words such as these in your mind as you inhale.

I breathe in the essence of the tree.
Let this purify and bring me vitality.

Hold the breath for about four seconds. Then breathe out slowly, emptying your lungs. Say in your mind while exhaling:

I breathe out tiredness
and all distress.
Let the leaves transmute them.
When they fall to earth
Let earthworms compost them.
Let this feed the tree I bless.

Repeat this cycle three times, beginning 'I breathe in the essence of the tree.'

It takes time to learn to synchronize the words with the breath pattern but after a while it becomes easy.

An experienced witch will see the potential in this simple spell as plants have varying magical properties. For example, the gorse could be approached for prosperity, allowing you to breathe in the essence of good fortune and success and breathe out bad luck and poverty. The wild rose can be approached for the essence of love, breathing out loneliness and so on. Of course, such spells do not have the glamour of a formal rite, done in a magic circle with all the trappings. But they do allow us to make mutually beneficial connections between the wild world (as represented by the tree) and human civilization (as represented by ourselves and our need). They are also, if done on a regular basis, surprisingly effective.

In a spell such as that of blessing and being blessed, there is a chance to be at one with the World Wood. This puts a witch where she or he has always needed to be – in the position of valued member of the community of all beings. Neither a parasite nor a vandal (even though human beings are often vandalistic to trees) but a magical creature whose problems and disharmonies, as well as skills and creativity, are a valid part of the cycle of creation. Of use to the land and the trees because transmutable.

The hedge witch, or any practitioner of natural magic, can take up this position on behalf of humanity, since this is what hedge witches traditionally do. They mediate between the spirits of the natural world and the human community. They may do this in many different ways once the principles underlying this kind of work have been understood. At this stage in history, it may be a more necessary kind of magic than it ever has been before.

The practice of 'tree breathing' described above also teaches a natural alchemy, since earthworms play as vital a role in it as the flowers and breezes. There is a lesson here in magic as well as in biology. This much I have learned from my faerie teacher to whom such matters as faerie philosophy are a real cause for enthusiasm. (She is a spirit contact, a teaching familiar who has been with me for many lifetimes.)

Natural magic asks you to honour the part played by all in the natural world, even those whom you don't find attractive, such as bacteria and worms. These are the agents of purification. They hasten and transform processes of rottenness and decay, breaking down what is unhealthy or dead, transforming it. By their work, what was unclean is purified, becoming the nourishment for new life – compost. They have true worth. They sustain life on Earth. All beings have a part to play in the magic of life through evolution. Some seem ugly and some beautiful but each type has a role.

She seems to be saying that acceptance of interdependence with all beings (whether they are rose or worm) is the foundation for any healthy magical power – and for living. But it is one thing to meditate on these matters, another to live by them, acknowledging that our dependence on trees and all the natural world is the foundation for our lives. If I, as a hedge witch, lived by this, I should be a magical guardian for the trees in my area, shouldn't I? I should honour my alliance with them, both as a hedge witch and as a living being on planet Earth. I am very aware of what I owe local trees and never more so than recently, since I failed to honour that debt. I was distracted by personal worries and when the trees of my own locality needed my help, I let them down.

This year, in the town where I live, around two hundred

trees were cut down, in an area called Summerleaze, to make way for the building of a supermarket carpark. These included mature oak, ash, beech, yew and Scot's pine. The one spell that I cast failed to save them, as did the townspeople's petition, which was signed by thousands of people. Neither were the trees saved by the magical efforts of other local witches nor by the courage of eco-warriors, who camped amongst them.

I think that for the rest of my life I will regret that I did not try harder to save those trees. I have a lasting sense of shame and a lot of unassuaged grief about their destruction. But to have had a chance of saving them, I would have needed to cast spells frequently and to make the matter a true priority. After all, there was a huge, national supermarket chain behind the chainsaws. Let us call them STAWMS, a word made from the initial letters of most of the supermarket chains in Britain. In this instance, as in many others, they know who they are.

The world needs many more hedge witches. I think that is the bottom line. Those of us who are working to heal and protect the environment magically – whether we call ourselves hedge witches or give the role some other name – are spread too thinly. In all lands on Earth, we are needed to protect local trees and also to help bespell for the rainforests on which the world depends. This is vital work.

According to a recent report in *The Independent* newspaper, dated 14 May 2007, deforestation now results in more carbon emissions than all cars and plane travel put together. This is because of slashing and burning. Smokestacks can be seen from space above the world's poorest countries, who see no choice in the matter, for lack of economic assistance by the developed countries. The information in the article came from the Oxford Global Canopy Programme, an alliance of the world's leading rainforest scientists. They say it is the biggest environmental issue we face today.

My shame and horror at the destruction of local West Country trees have, in the end, produced good results. One of these is that I now cast a spell for the increase of trees, daily. It's a simple, informal piece of enchantment plus sympathetic magic.

Briefly, I light a candle and stand before an altar to the Mother Goddess and Father God. I say some prayers for all humanity, in respect of our need for the healing of our relationship with the natural world. Then I say this.

Spell for the Increase of Trees

*In the names of Mother Earth
and the Green God of trees
let all the world's woodland
increase and increase.*

*As the word 'trees' comes from my mouth
let new trees come from the Earth a millionfold
to East and West and North and South
and all throughout.
Let them be in harmony with one another
and with all species and be protected.
And let them stand and stand
to live out their natural life span
and reproduce their kind.*

*By all the powers of wind, light, rain, land and wraith
and by three times three,
more trees, more trees, more trees,
more trees, more trees, more trees,
more trees, more trees, more trees,
So may it be.*

During the Cold War, I often did such simple magic for the cause of World Peace, as did countless numbers of witches and non-witches, worldwide. Millions joined their prayers, spells and affirmations for this common cause. As a hedge witch, a wand wielder and broomstick rider, I propose that the same kind of effort could be made for the World Wood. However tiny each spell may appear of itself, it adds up to something impressive if done daily. Imagine the wonderful result if large numbers of us were working for trees, aligned with the World Wood to preserve and increase the trees. We can work with many familiar spirits even when apparently alone. We can join forces with many spirits – elementals, elves, ancestors. We can design many rites and brand new spells based on new insights. We can, therefore, make all the difference.

In the following chapters I shall suggest rites for making alliances with helpful spirits and spells to banish harm as well as bring increase. The work is not solemn or rigid in its approach. It requires dedication but also zest and creativity.

Chapter 3

ᵺedge Witchcraft for the Present Day

The hedge witch of old, the *hagazissa*, worked to keep the balance between the human community and 'wild spirit', by which was meant the domain of nature spirits, elves, place spirits, elementals and all kinds of natural untamed forces. This may often have meant the need to ensure the survival of a fragile human community, beset by many threats from the natural world, such as hungry animals. In today's world, with humanity so much in control (and so little at peace), at least in First World countries, the situation is rather different. So we often need to reinterpret old traditions and magical practices in the light of our knowledge that much wilderness (the domain of wild spirit) has been destroyed or is under threat.

Our task is to use our imagination to find magical ways to mend the human relationship with nature. Not only that but to help bring evolution to human concepts of nature. Too many still see nature primarily as an enemy, instead of seeing Her as our Mother and our home and as a realm of which we are part, indivisible from, and interdependent with. In relation to liminal places such as hedgerows or forest edges, and to trees, shrubs, herbs and things made from them for magical uses, such as wands, broomsticks and herbal potions, we can reinvent hedge witchcraft and, ourselves, be reinvented by doing so. This is a challenge, a work of the soul for the adventurous type, the explorer. It's a far cry from selling love charms or curses against your neighbour's cattle. But it may be close to the very first most ancient type of hedge witchcraft – a pure attempt to make friends with wild spirits, gain familiars, live at one, in co-operation.

For us, today, it is Native Americans who seem to embody that approach, at least, mythically. But all over the world, in every culture, on each continent, there were people who had the same idea. In Europe, some were called *hagazissas*. They were those upon the border between humanity and all nature, between villagers and the faeries, between the living and the dead. And they made of it a place of unity, having one foot in each camp, whatever the conflict or polarity.

Nowadays, the perceived conflict is between science and the soul – or between expediency and a sense of the sacred. The green hedge witch transcends the boundary, envisioning a world where science can reveal and serve the sacred because benignly serving all.

So what does it mean to sit in a hedgerow or forest edge for magical purposes?

Some European hedgerows are so old that they were planted in the Neolithic period when most land was heavily forested, home to wolves, bears and wild boar, amongst other creatures. The hedge was a boundary designed to keep things out (such as dangerous animals and people) rather than solely to keep things in (such as livestock). This places the hedge witch between the civilized and the untamed, and uniting them in some way – in co-operation or compromise – for the good of the people. She or he could mediate between the spirits of wild creatures, elemental forces or places and human beings. The hedge witch also went beyond the hedge in search of herbs for magical uses and to confer with faerie presences, ancestral spirits and shining ones.

These last are the most highly evolved of spirit presences. They are mediators of health, harmony and well-being. The world calls them angels, associating them with Judaism and Christianity. But they were and are also known to Pagans in many indigenous traditions. In Northern Europe they have been known as light-elves. However, these Pagan angels are wild and free. The piousness associated with Christian angels in Britain (since Victorian times, anyway) is very far from their behaviour. They hold the vision of ideal ways of being, of being in joy and harmony. Just as necessary to life and health are their cousins, the dark-elves, of whom I shall write more presently.

The hedge witch, having gone through the hedge, could return with magical solutions to any problem and with information from many kinds of guiding spirits.

From a twenty-first-century perspective, it seems to me that the practice of linking the known human realm with the unknown, the mystery, could require a linking of two aspects of our own minds, perhaps the two hemispheres of the human brain. This brings, in effect, a connection of rational, linear, everyday consciousness with the intuitive, psychic and trans-rational.

Then, as now, an 'altered state' would have been essential to the development of powers that are used in magic. To sit in or astride a hedge means not only to be between two realms but to partake of each. The art of the hedge sitter has always been to combine rational with psychic consciousness. To put it another way, this means we can enter faerieland with our wits about us and return in safety. We certainly can reach that state in which a spell can seem to speak itself through our mouths without any effort, spontaneously. I can vouch for that. We can read a landscape as a whole series of spirit messages from Mother Earth. We can meet psychically with our familiars and faerie teachers, gaining assistance and working with them in co-operation for mutual benefit. We can do such things as present-day hedge witches by using old ideas and techniques creatively. They are the fruits of unity between the rational and the psychic aspects of ourselves and of the world, the results of an altered state of consciousness.

That altered state is reached by spells involving hedgerows or forest edges or other liminal places and/or woodland products like staffs or broomsticks. There are so many ways to interpret these ancient themes that we are quite spoilt for choice! And I think that this may have always been so, anywhere on Earth, for our ancestors, too. I say this because I think that beginner witches can often make the mistake of thinking that there was once a 'real' kind of hedge witchcraft – but only *one* kind. And that we must copy it or fail to be authentic. Tradition does count. It is our foundation. But many styles of what we may broadly term hedge witchcraft may have been practised throughout Northern Europe and even throughout the world, throughout the ages. There have been many ways of bestriding boundaries, walking 'between the worlds' and working with wands or broomsticks or herbal potions. And many more ways of casting a spell than we can now shake a stick at! (Which seems a good saying, really, for a wand bearer.)

There are some interesting examples of the hedge witch's practices in folklore and mythology. One is simply the old belief that if you walk between two trees you can

enter the Otherworld (that is, enter faerie). Tradition does not tell us which species of tree these may be nor where they are. Fundamentally, I think they may be any two trees anywhere on this Earth, providing you walk between them in the right spirit. First, you must speak an appropriate spell. I have tried this many times and it is successful, producing an altered state that varies between being so light you can carry on normal tasks such as taking your dog for a walk and so deep that you can hold prolonged (psychic) conversations with elves. One thing it does not do is remove choice. You can remain in charge and snap back to everyday consciousness at need, any time that *you* like. Here is the type of spell that I use and you are welcome to try it, too.

Spell for Increased Awareness of Elves

May I now walk between
as though through a door
from unseen to seen.
May the human realms be behind me
and faerie realms before.
In the names of the Greenwood
Goddess and God,
I go between tree and tree.
May I now enter the Otherworld
in joy and safety.

The Greenwood Lady and Lord in whose names you cast the spell are Goddess and God of the whole World Wood, by which we mean the realm of nature at its most vibrant and magical. Particular names by which you may know them are Freya and Freyr, Marian and Robin or Isis and Osiris. Throughout the world, they have had many names and titles in many lands. If you know what these are in your area, you may prefer to use them in order to honour local tradition. In any case, they are deities of Nature as the untamed revelation of Mystery and manifestation of sacredness. They have many faces and forms here on Earth and in other dimensions as well as our own. If you are not comfortable using names for them, it is much better to use titles, such as 'Greenwood Lady and Lord' rather than to speak words uncertainly.

Another tradition – from British folklore – states that we witches have hawthorn hedges at the bottom of our gardens. I wish! For those who did or do have one, going through the hedge to collect herbs or to enter 'the wild spirit domain' must have been a powerful experience as well as a thorny one! But why a hawthorn hedge, especially?

An answer may lie in Arthurian mythology, where it is said that Nimue and Merlin retreated into a hawthorn tower which she created by her magic. Late and distorted versions of that story say that she did it to imprison him. In the earliest versions, she merely aimed to create a sanctuary in which he could work his magic and practise divination without disturbance. Could this place have been a hawthorn bower? If so, could the story have been based on practices of the hedge witch, the sitter within the hedge or the sacred grove? A hawthorn hedge would be a place of great magic in any case. In faerie tradition, the thorny plants, such as hawthorn and rose, can either prevent or grant access into the Otherworld. This is shown in many tales, including those as diverse as the French 'Sleeping Beauty' and the Scottish 'Janet and Tam Lin'. Hawthorn and wild rose can create portals into the land of faerie or guard that doorway against intruders.

In all such tales or pieces of folklore, the gaining of entry into a more magical place (or aspect of life) is achieved through connection with hedges or trees.

As I said, it is my experience that such practices really work to produced altered states of consciousness in which we can enter what may be – or what we may call – faerie. This is the point. They produce subtle altered states. What's more, I have walked physically into another or parallel dimension, leaving this one behind. Outrageous though it may sound, such things are possible. But they are rare. It is my belief they can only be done with the permission and help of elves, especially of those we may term 'wards', those who guard such portals. The faerie gates are not to be stormed by force of will nor passed in stealth by devious spells. Anyone trying it would do so at their own peril. I *don't* recommend it. No, the proper course for a hedge witch, when it comes to physical entry into the faerie realm, is to wait politely for invitations. It is not necessary to have that kind of adventure to cast spells, anyway.

I and many, many hedge witches have often walked between trees or stood in a liminal place of some kind and entered a psychic Otherworld. Then nature spirits, elves and, sometimes, discarnate people or ghostly animals can be glimpsed with eyes wide open (not closed as when visualizing something). Conversations can also be held, mind to mind (telepathically), with familiars and other spirits. Otherworldly sounds such as bells or music can sometimes be heard. Also, scents for which there is no earthly source can sometimes be smelt. In this heightened state, magic can be done most powerfully.

This is not so much a walking through into another world as an entering into increased awareness of subtle dimensions *already here*. We don't walk away from the magic of Middle Earth (the world in which we all live). It remains all around us but we walk into a deeper and stronger awareness of it and of such wild spirit presences who may be found in woodland or hedgerow, orchard or garden, hilltop or moorland, riverbank, lakeside or seashore. We gain some awareness of all this while retaining full consciousness of our physical, earthly surroundings. After all, our spirits have chosen lives in Middle Earth, in human form. We are here to serve this everyday world to the best of our magical abilities.

As hedge witches, we increase our own awareness of

the presence of spirit in nature on behalf of the human community. This acknowledgement of sacredness in all the natural world is vital and may be the key to healing the human relationship with all of nature.

We gradually learn to achieve this awareness at liminal places, symbolically and imaginatively, by linking the brain's two hemispheres and, perhaps, by other bio-chemical and neural responses unknown to us. To help ourselves, we make a small ritual out of our passing through a hedge/forest edge/wooden gateway or out of sitting astride a wooden broom or staff. And we use spells whose rhythmic and semi-hypnotic patterns and rhymes all help to produce the desired effect. And we use *imagination*.

On top of all this, we are doubtless changed by prox-imity to trees. Their auras and subtle energies can have a magical effect upon us. Not for nothing are woods connected with faeries and witches (as well as outlaws) in popular belief. Trees, on a dark night, can seem to offer both shelter and menace. On a bright day, a wooded area seems a place of adventure, seduction and exploration. We feel challenged by trees, more alive, psychically, because of them. Trees rarely fail to have some emotional effect upon us. Psychologically, they are associated with hidden and wild impulses. (Even the trees of a dense, unruly, riotous British hedgerow can suggest all of this, especially when they are in full leaf.)

Another possible explanation, on a biological level, for a witch's state of consciousness is that we may be achiev-ing a link between the forebrain (the site of mentation) and the hindbrain (which is involved with instincts and dream states). In any case, whether the links are between left and right hemispheres or between the forebrain and hindbrain or the mind and soul, and whether achieved by the effects of trees, spells and rituals or help from the elves, or a combination of these, they do bring awareness of a more subtle dimension, a real magic.

However I am not suggesting that the words 'subtle dimension' or 'Otherworld' or 'faerie realm' are a fancy way of referring to the brain's right hemisphere or the hindbrain or only to a visionary aspect of human psychology. What I am saying is that it is with the transrational aspects of the mind or the brain that we can know the realm of faerie. We can then become active within a subtle but objective form of reality, one which is always present but which is usually beyond our range of perception.

The crux of hedge witchcraft or any other magical practice is that the rational and transrational must somehow be connected within us so that they work together as one. This is what distinguishes magic from, say, a dream or from a drug-induced fantasy. In most dreams, the transrational mind (and the pineal gland) are very active but rational consciousness is suspended.

Let me sum up these ideas about liminal places and altered consciousness by being practical for a moment. From a hedge witch's point of view we really do need a hedge or a line of trees or some kind of plant boundary, even a wooden fence, which divides two differing types of terrain – or can be perceived as doing so. In that way, the symbolism of the technique is grounded in physical reality. Therefore our hearts can feel convinced by it and our minds can respond accordingly. We need, like the *hagazissa* of old, to face towards a place which is more, somehow, otherworldly, than that which lies behind us. That which lies before should suggest to our physical senses a place of more beauty or more wildness. This can be done in many ways and here are some obvious examples.

Liminal Places for the Hedge Witch

1 Stand in any hedge or row of trees or any boundary of lavender or other herbs or of bamboo (depending upon where you are in the world). Face towards an area of fields, farmland or forest and away from your town or village.

2 Stand in a hedge around a beautiful orchard, facing into it and away from the 'ordinary' fields. If there are no hedge gaps so that you cannot stand within the hedgerow, stand in the orchard with your back against the hedge or sit close to it.

3 Sit or stand within a boundary. (I know the term is 'hedge sitter', implying that you should do your magic while sitting down. Sometimes you will. But it is not always practical. Sit or stand according to your own needs and inclinations.) Face towards a range of hills or mountains, however distant, and away from the more densely populated lowland.

4 Sit or stand in a row of trees on the edge of a nature reserve, facing into it.

5 Sit or stand in a row of trees on the edge of a forest. Face the forest and not the fields or town near to it.

6 If in a town or city, place yourself in or near the boundary around a park or a beautiful garden. Face towards the heart of the garden with the urban streets behind you.

7 When working indoors, for reasons of ill-health, cold weather or simple choice, create a symbolic boundary

by sitting between two wooden staffs, wands or even twigs. Place nearby a few objects of natural beauty, to symbolize the realm of wild spirit. Sit or stand facing towards them or towards a shrine or altar which you have made to celebrate nature, wild spirit and Mystery. The objects you choose for such a place could be feathers, special candles scented with aromatherapy oils, spring water in a glass bowl, stones or crystals, flowers, fossils, pieces of amber or jet or coal, moss, small logs or bits of tree bark and ivy or house plants growing in pots.

8 Last but not least, you can create a hedgerow within psychic reality by visualizing one. Place it upon the very edge of a village or town with fields and perhaps a forest beyond it. In imagination, you can sit within it or pass through or even fly over it on your broomstick. This gives you an inner place in which to practise natural magic or to commune with guiding spirits. In a later chapter, I will describe a sequence of spells which can be done in an inner, imagined hedgerow as well as in a physical one. (This type of thing, a psychic spellcasting, is sometimes known as an 'astral working'. It is most effective and also functions as preparation for work done in an actual hedge or forest edge. Psychic and magical skills which you have built up in an inner hedgerow are transferable to a physical site and they bring confidence.)

Here is a simple rite of hedge witchcraft. Stand in a hedgerow gap or forest edge. Place your non-dominant foot forward. For right-handed people, this is the left foot. It is the right foot for left-handed people. In any event, this is the one that is said to be ruled by the brain's right hemisphere, the *intuitive* mind. By doing this, you are enacting, ritually, the fact of having one foot in faerie and one in the domain of humanity. Alternatively, you can raise your non-dominant foot and stand on one leg. This is an old shamanic posture and is found in many traditions – including that of the Freemasons, so far as I know. It enacts the same idea but can be much harder to maintain for long periods. Say something like this.

Spell For Altered Consciousness

I stand between the worlds.
Before me, let there lie all the bright realm
of wild spirit. Behind, all the solid realm
of humanity, which has nurtured me
from my birth.

Before, behind,
unknown and known,
wild heart and mind,
the mystery and the mundane,
realm of the elves and that of humankind
now be at one
within me and in all creation,
to the healing of all beings on this Earth.

Pause and then add,

In the names of the Greenwood Lady and Lord, may I now
receive spirit guidance about [for example] magic to heal the rela-
tionship between humanity and nature. May I learn now how
harmony can be restored.

Sit or stand within the hedge and let your mind grow still. The question you have just asked is a huge one. It goes without saying that it does not rest with you or any one individual to heal humanity, single-handedly. However you may now gain understanding about some ways in which healing could occur and about some part, however seemingly small, which you may play in this. Do not rack your brains nor struggle in any way to find an answer. (In fact, you may receive one suddenly, later on, when the rite is over.) Just wait, in alert passivity, turning your mind to the mind of nature, Earth's mind, in the land upon which you stand. We are the children of Earth, each one of us. Humanity is Her dominant species, a much-favoured and precocious child with massive potential. She wants to conserve us as well as all other species. For all its faults, this child is loved and the Earth has invested much hope and pride in it. How can this child be assisted to grow up and relearn connectedness with the rest of creation, the rest of the natural world, on a mature basis? Let your mind grow still.

After a while, you may find that images begin to form in your mind or that an inner voice can be heard. Look and listen carefully for any insight about how you may, as a hedge witch, assist psychically and magically, with this work of human evolution. (Or with any other aspect of healing the relationship between human needs and those of the land and all species.) Do not strive to find the answers but simply put the question to Mother Earth and to the elves, to the land itself, and to nearby trees, inside your mind.

You may sit or stand to do this for a few minutes or for a few hours but should only remain as long as you're comfortable and as long as you feel that your awareness is deepening, psychically. The act of asking this question, respectfully, on behalf of the human community, is, in itself, a psychic healing because it remakes the lost connection between the human mind and the mind of wild spirit, which is a sacred connection. Move on when you feel like doing so.

Pass through the hedge and go for a walk. Wander wherever you feel inclined to go. Notice each sight and sound in the landscape as though it were a message from the mind of Mother Earth, as indeed it is. You may not understand these messages on a rational level but your soul will absorb them, easily. (People who practise natural magic can become very sensitive to all kinds of subtle messages, both good and bad. That is why it is doubly important for us to balance distressing human messages – such as those from the news media – with more primal and creative messages from the natural world.) Every so often, it may occur to you to ask your question again. You may ask, for example, the spirit of a pool of water or of the passing clouds. You could ask a fox, a crow, a butter-fly. In this way, your question acquires a ritualistic aspect. 'Tree, what magic could heal the human relationship with nature?' And 'Hare, what magic could heal . . .' 'Snake, what magic could heal. . . ?'

The question itself becomes a kind of enchantment, bringing you into the mythic aspect of landscape and the world, for this kind of repetitious questioning is very old and is often found in faerie tales. In such tales people have all kinds of conversations with creatures and plants and even with inanimate objects, such as stones. To the ratio-nal mind, there is no wisdom in any creatures, let alone in trees or stones, so what is the point? But to the trans-rational mind, Earth's spirit is in every one of us and in all elemental things, such as wild animals, plants, places. And it must be remembered that Earth got on very well with-out any human guidance, for many millions of years, managing creative evolution, producing multitudes of species, adapting over and again to changing galactic conditions. She must know something! By asking those who are closer to Her in their hearts than are most human beings, we may learn something of natural wisdom.

Doubtless, a lot of people would say that this kind of thing is merely a trick, a device for contacting some submerged part of our own minds, our own wisdom. Because, of course, animals, plants and so on can't advise us. Anyway, what could they know? I don't agree. But it doesn't matter how we explain such magical techniques so long as they work. And they do work. But you may have to practise for a while if you are new to these things. You need to develop an unselfconscious, dreamy state of mind, and be calmly receptive. The ideas and insights gained in this way may feel tenuous at first but you should value them. Do not try too hard. Be relaxed and treat the whole thing as a creative experiment. In this way, you give your psychic faculties every chance.

When you feel you have wandered enough – both mentally and physically – return to the hedgerow and face the direction from which you came through the gap. Say something like this.

I return now to the human realm
of Middle Earth.
May the green mantle of natural magic
be around my shoulders, in spirit,
giving protection against every kind
of psychic harm.
Now, in the names of the Greenwood
Lady and Lord, may I step forth,
an emissary of wild spirit
within the everyday world.
May my psychic senses now return
to a state suitable for my human life.

The words 'green mantle' refer to the Earth's own covering of vegetation, alive with various kinds of enchantment, as are the leaves of trees when the wind blows through them. By saying such words (in the above context) you will invoke strong psychic protection from the Earth's own magical spirit. And you may be very glad about that for it is frequently the case that when we come back from such excursions the human world of bustling streets can seem very harsh. And indeed it is, in comparison with the elven world of a woodland or range of hills or riverside or wherever it is you have been.

Many humans have an atavistic fear of bad spirits, encountered in wild and lonely places, especially in the dark. Believe me, they are nothing to those that sometimes lurk in a modern city, feeding on human corruption and cruelty. As sensitivity increases in the trainee witch, she or he may find such presences or their psychic atmosphere depressing and draining. Therefore, I recommend some psychic protection such as the green mantle.

After your walk, it is often a good idea to conclude with some physical but easy activity, such as having a drink. Or to take a rest. This helps you to make the transition more easily into the everyday world. If you are inexperienced, it may not be a good idea to drive a car nor to use machinery, straight away. First, you need to be sure that you have returned to a rational, grounded consciousness. Usually, this takes just a few minutes but you do need to be aware that it could take longer.

Chapter 4

Charm against Harm

So far we have looked at the hedgerow as a symbolic boundary between the realm of humankind and that of wild spirit – the natural realm. *And* as a place where we can bring reason and intuition into a balanced state within ourselves. But there are many other ways in which we can interpret this theme of boundaries, not least in the currently fashionable way of using the word to denote anything which protects our own autonomy.

The first and most basic boundary for any one of us is that between our own self and all that we define as 'not self'. That which is 'not self' may begin with everything which is outside our own skin. An even more private and, we would like to think, inviolate area is, for each one of us, comprised of feelings, thoughts and that psychic area known as the soul. We make many distinctions, such as 'my body/your body', or 'my opinions/your opinions' or 'my spirituality/your feelings about my spirituality', in defining boundaries around ourselves.

We sometimes need, in today's phraseology, to 'maintain our boundaries' with efficiency, patrolling our symbolic hedge or forest edge. Everyone knows that if you let someone else tell you what to think and who to be, quite soon you can't call your soul your own. Your life as a free individual is curtailed or even finished. We also know that such abuse is fairly commonplace in this world. People attempt to do this to one another in families, in love affairs, at work and in any number of social groups. It also happens within religious and cultural life. Sometimes this psychological abuse is backed up by violence.

In the past, part of our job as hedge witches would have been to maintain boundaries by psychic means. What I mean by this is that we would have been expected to help keep the community safe from psychic attack by bad spirits as well as from any aggressive magic done by persons from other communities. (In fact, this would have been the job of many practitioners of magic, whether they were or were not known as hedge sitters. Priestesses or priests, the local shaman, Druid, wise woman or cunning man, all would have been expected to do this work from time to time.)

In Northern Europe, such protection magic was achieved with the help of local earth spirits, who were called 'wards'. But there could be more to it in times of crisis. A legendary example is that of the witches of Britain who got together to raise a storm to sink the Spanish Armada, thus helping to protect their country.

As well as protecting boundaries, hedge witches welcome people through gaps in various symbolic boundaries. We can use magic to invite others into either our lives or those of the people in our communities. An obvious example of this would be the casting of a love spell. Other examples of what we might bring in or bring across boundaries could be new opportunities for learning, wealth based on exchange with other communities, new ideas, friends, technologies, or medicines involving herbs from other parts of the world.

Traditionally, a witch cast a spell when someone asked

for help and not otherwise. Exceptions to this rule would be spells done for those who can't ask – for example, animals, very small children, plants or places. It is all too easy to believe we are casting useful and helpful spells when, in fact, the unwitting recipient would call it inter-ference. We can ourselves be guilty of cutting across someone else's boundaries if this rule is not remembered.

To sum up, witches need to know how to balance factions on either side of a boundary *and* how to keep something outside a boundary and how to bring from beyond a boundary those things which enrich life and allow creativity.

Here are some examples of boundaries which some-times need to be maintained and sometimes to be crossed. In each case, there is a symbolic hedgerow or forest edge around at least one of the polarities.

1 the individual	other people
2 our own community	other communities/ethnic groups
3 our own beliefs	beliefs of others (social, reli-gious, political etc.)
4 our own nationality/ race	another nationality/race
5 humanity	the rest of the natural world
6 the living	the dead and the unborn
7 human reality	any parallel dimension or faerie reality

There is plenty of work for any hedge witch in today's world, working to help create the right conditions on such borders as those listed – and on others, too. But how is it done? Here is an example.

Rite of the Hedgerow

Stand in a gap within a hedge, or at a woodland edge, or within the line of seaweed thrown up on the beach at high tide, or between two trees, or sit on a wooden stile or fence. Alternatively, you can work indoors. If you do stay inside, stand facing an altar or shrine which you have made to the powers of nature. This could be a small wooden table or shelf or anything else that you feel is suitable. Arrange upon it a symbolic tree to denote the World Wood.

Upon my own altar, I have a constructed tree made of twigs in a vase. It has embroidered leaves and flowers made of felt. The fruits, supposed to be apples in this case, are painted wooden beads. Many bird feathers are in the vase among the twigs and I have hung a silver moon pendant among the branches as well as decorating them with coloured ribbons. You could create something of your own or you may prefer to place a framed painting or photograph of a tree on your altar. Add a couple of candles in natural-looking pottery or glass holders. You may also want to keep your wand there when you have one. (Later, I will explain how to make and consecrate your own wand or staff.) Feathers, a bowl of spring water or a shell and pebbles or fossils may be placed there, too. Thus, you will have a representation of each one of the five basic elements in the World Wood – air, fire, water, earth and wraith or ether. The fifth element can be represented by a length of white or undyed cord. In magical tradition, cords and strings symbolize 'threads of fate', the web of destiny. These weavings are made of 'spirit stuff', wraith, a ghost substance from Earth's most subtle dimension which underlies and gives form to the people, events, creatures and places we see all around us. You might say that wraith is the psychic material from which the Goddess of Fate spins all her yarn.

If indoors, begin by turning off all phones and clearing away any distracting objects, such as newspapers or unanswered letters. Light the candles. Stand facing the altar, between two staffs – small logs or twigs placed to make a symbolic hedge or boundary. Whether indoors or out, place your non-dominant foot forward and say the following spell.

Spell for Communion with Wild Spirits

Let me stand as though in a hedgerow
between the worlds.
Let this boundary be a place of union.
In the names of the Lady and Lord of natural magic,
They who are Goddess and God
within the World Wood,
let this boundary be a place of union
between the wild spirit domain
and all that is human.
By all the powers of beauty and truth and love
let this boundary be a meeting place
for all friendly spirits who are here,
to the left, to the right,
before and behind and below and above.
Let this boundary be a place of union.

Pause and then continue, saying something like this.

And let this boundary
be also within me,
between the elven realms and humanity,
as a place of union,
to the healing of myself
and all creation.

Now pick up a birch twig – which you will need to have brought with you and placed within easy reach. If there is no birch available near where you live, you can use a herb with a reputation for psychic cleansing. A sprig of sage, thyme or rosemary would do very well. Juniper is powerful but prickly to handle. Bay laurel or cedar are also good choices. Say the following or something like it.

Spell for Psychic Purification

As any tree upon a boundary
let me be cleansed by the elements
now and in all my days to come
from every kind of harm set free.

Let me be cleansed by wind and light
and rain and land of every blight
and cleansed by wraith that is fresh and bright.
So fall from me to Earth's deep mill
all that is stale, outworn or ill
by natural law and my own will –
there to be changed by spirit powers
to that which feeds life –
fruit, leaves and flowers.

Using the birch or cedar twig or herbal sprig, sweep through the area round your own body, the space known as your own aura. In its most concentrated form this extends for a foot or two, all around you in every direction. Sweep from above the crown of your head right down to the ground on the front of your body and do the same behind (to the best of your ability). Then sweep down each side of yourself.

On another occasion, the above spell may be used for someone else rather than for yourself. Just change the words appropriately. It may also be used for a creature or plant. The birch, cedar or herb sweeping brings an immediate freshening-up. The words of the spell are designed to bring a deeper and more lasting form of psychic purification on any exposure to earth, water, sun, fresh air or a wild green area – for example while going for a walk or while gardening.

You may have wondered what was meant by the phrase 'Earth's deep mill'. This is a metaphor for the land's processes of composting corrupt matter, rotting it down, transforming it into new nourishment for living plants. Psychic material, too, can be composted, recycling negative energy and turning it into a source of creativity. Thus, we do not just dump what is harmful but cast a spell to transform it.

Such purification rids us of psychic residue of things like stress, whether generated by ourselves or by others in our vicinity. In order to understand this, you need to know that to a witch feelings have a psychic power and reality, as well as an emotional and biochemical one. They can generate – on the psychic level – things like colours, scents, temperatures and textures. Sometimes we need to be cleansed of the psychic effect of destructive or inharmonious. feelings, such as bitterness, guilt, cynicism, frustration and deceit. Purification can also deal with any unclean psychic energy, such as that left behind in a room by a devotee of pornography.

A toxic psychic atmosphere, for instance one that is generated by spite, cruelty or malice, can attract spirits of a like nature, creating a seriously unpleasant and often terrifying atmosphere that can be felt by anyone with any kind of sensitivity. Seriously troubled spots are best left to experts and not dealt with by the trainee witch. However it is good to practise psychic cleansing around ourselves and our own homes in order to avoid a build-up of anything generated by both others and ourselves. Psychic overload, even simple stress, can adversely affect your health and bring on fatigue, especially if you are psychically sensitive, the open type. In fact, psychic purification makes as much sense as physical hygiene. It is a very, very old practice, found in most magical/spiritual traditions, worldwide. The foregoing is just one example of how a hedge witch might go about it. Here is something else you can do to protect boundaries.

Step forward through the boundary gap and into the orchard, garden, wood or water's edge or whatever you face. If indoors, do not step right up to the altar but move into the centre of the area in which you are working. Turn around sunwise (deosil) upon the spot. That is, turn around to your right, in a clockwise direction. Do not do it so many times that you become dizzy. While slowly circling, call on the elemental spirits to assist you with magic. You can say something very simple, such as the following.

I call to you, elemental spirits
of air, fire, water, earth and wraith.
Come to me. Bless my spells with success.
Hail and welcome!

Or you can say something more elaborate, like this.

Spell to Call upon Elemental Spirits for Assistance

Let me be allied with the wind.
Let me be aided by bright flame
and be befriended by the rain
and work with spirits of the land
and with those who tend the Veil.
Come to me, elementals, hail!
Empower each spell. On you I call.
Come bless with power my voice and hand.

The 'Veil' mentioned here is a symbolic reference to the boundaries of the fifth element, which is a/ether or wraith (chi, prana, ond).

I suggest this lengthier, second invocation of elemental spirits so that you can become clear that they are not an abstract matter. These spirits exist in the natural world within its subtle, psychic aspect. However you do not have to learn this or other long spells suggested by me, in order to be a practising hedge witch. Magical work is easier if you do have many basic, frequently used spells committed to memory, but you do not have to have that. Once you know what is required, such as a psychic purification, you can improvise on the spot. You can use your own words and use very few of them if that is what you prefer to do. Remember, the themes, symbols and practices of hedge witchcraft are very, very old. But the words that you use to call on the spirits can be as fresh as today. When they are simple and straight from your heart they are invariably effective. Mine are suggestions. That is all.

Faerie contacts of other kinds than the elementals are possible for a hedge witch and there will be more on this in a later chapter. However, we will next proceed to an invocation of the deities – the Goddess and God of natural magic, who are, in fact, the divine presences within the natural world, in all creation.

Step forward to face your altar, if you are working indoors. If outside, go to a tree or clump of reeds or whatever it is you have chosen to represent an area or species for your magical work on behalf of trees.

Raise your arms from the elbow with the palms of your hands facing forward, in the traditional gesture of invocation.

Invocation of Deities

Hail, great Lady and gracious Lord
of natural magic
in the World Wood,
You who bring life, death and rebirth
to serve evolution, the common good.
Bless each spell
that brings a healing
or a truth-revealing
making well.
I bring these offerings,
to serve all,
my heart and soul,
my wordless call.

Hum or chant an improvised tune, projecting it, in imagination, to the Goddess and God of natural magic, whom you have just invoked.

These deities may be pictured as rainbow light around a green tree or as a moonlit pool and an antlered stag or as a beautiful, strong woman and man or in many another form. Actually, they are female and male aspects of the life force, which is in all beings and everywhere. They are both general and particular. That is, they are in you and me and also in everything, throughout the natural world. They are both spiritual and material and, in fact, they are spirit *as* matter. They are the mystery of the universe, powers of magic, raw and sacred.

That which we offer to the deities is said to be returned to us, transformed. So our hearts and souls and powers of enchantment become more aligned with the patterns and tides of the natural world by such practices as the above, especially if done frequently. It is important to remember that anything we offer the deities should be the best we have and also our own to give, conveying a real part of ourselves. An offering such as wine poured out on the ground, if it was bought and easily afforded, may not be so effective in increasing our alignment with the deities as is a song, however halting, or a handmade object (or wine made by ourselves). This is forgotten all too easily.

It is a good idea, at this point, to state the purpose of your rite to the elemental spirits and deities. In this partic-ular instance, you could say something like the following.

I am here to work magic for the benefit of trees. First, I shall cast a spell to rid them of harm.

Do not be worried by the next bit. You are about to utter a curse but it is for benign purposes – not to be confused with an ill-wish. Cursing is an ancient magical practice and designed to cause something to wither away until it is gone. There is a famous Anglo-Saxon example called 'Charm against the Wen', in which the object cursed is a tumour. Indeed, curses can be used against many illnesses and various problems. They should never be used against people – or other creatures – to destroy their well-being or happiness. No good can come of malice or spite. They harm the aggressor as much as the victim because we are

all obliged to live in the resonance of what we do, however
secretly. Spite attracts spite. The following curse is for
healing purposes.

You will need a very small piece of paper torn from a
piece of junk mail, to symbolize the abuse of trees (the
world's trees being cut down to advertise things we can
usually manage rather better without). Alternatively, you
could use a bit of tropical hardwood, a small sliver from a
box or garden bench (to symbolize rainforests, the lungs of
the world, being chopped down to produce souvenirs and
garden furniture). If you are working for water plants, you
might use a piece of rotten food or, again, paper (to
symbolize the World Ocean being used as a dumping
ground for the masses of rubbish produced in the restau-
rants of ships). These things are examples. I can think of
quite a few that are more distressing. However, you will
need something that *can* symbolize all abuse of trees and
yet is biodegradable for this spell.

Hold the paper or wood in your hand. Turn around
three times, to your left (moonwise, widdershins). Say the
following.

Curse against Harm to Trees

In the names of the Greenwood Lady and Lord,
may the health of woodland be restored
by this cursing of all harm done to trees.
Let all abuse of trees now cease.
Let it all wither and shrink and fail
like an aged branch or leaves in the fall,
until it is gone, with harm to no one –
to no living creature nor any species.
By the powers of rain, light, wind, land and wraith,
let all abuse of trees wither away
until it entirely cease

as rots junk mail, piece by piece.
So may it be.

Obviously, you can change the words of the above curse to suit your purposes. If you were holding a sliver of teak from a garden table, you could say 'as rots this piece of wood' instead of 'as rots junk mail' in the penultimate line. If working by the seashore, you could say 'may the health of seaweed be restored by this cursing of harm done to the seas' instead of the second and third lines of the curse as given here. Now that you know the formula, you can use it at your discretion. But be careful.

It is never, ever morally justified nor constructive to curse another person nor any type, class, race or gender *or species* simply because you think the world would be a better place without them. All have their part to play and it is a much better idea to curse the demons of greed, intolerance, spite or aggression (or other bad qualities) which may possess them. Each type and every individual is here as a unique expression of Goddess or God and is needed in creation. To use cursing to give anyone a hard time or to destroy them or their creativity is unwise magic. We are better employed in the service of healing. To curse the abuse and all its causes and leave the abuser/s free to be transformed and healed is an approach that can only do good.

From all this, I hope it is now clear that a curse can be a form of healing in itself. It does not have to be an unkind spell – and need not be an ill-wish!

Always include in a curse – or in *any* spell – these words: 'Let such and such [the aim of your spell] come to be, with harm to no one.' Then the success of the spell is conditional upon no one being harmed in the process. This really is extremely important if you want to practise hedge witchcraft with integrity, as I am sure you do.

Otherwise, to put it mildly, we natural magicians could be no better than terrorists because our spells could hurt other people.

Follow the curse against abuse with a blessing to bring to trees an increase in numbers. Place your hands against a tree – or hold a piece of seaweed if working for sea plants. If indoors, visualize a tree on which to place your hands for this spell or touch a leaf or twig representing the woodland or particular tree species or trees in general, depending upon the chosen aim of your spell on this occasion. The following is an example of what you might then say and is a blessing constructed along traditional lines, according to the rules of spellcraft.

A Blessing for Trees

In the names of the Lady and Lord
of natural magic and the World Wood,
let all native trees in the land increase
in harmony with all other species,
harming none under moon, stars or sun.
Trees, may you and your living kind,
all native trees, increase nine times nine,
to reproduce in woodland and forest.
By all the powers of wind, light, rain, land and wraith,
by three times three,
increase, increase, increase native trees,
increase, increase, increase native trees,
increase, increase, increase native trees
in all lands on Earth.
So may it be.

This spell is ambitious to say the least. It is a blessing of increase for all the Earth's trees, stressing that each type should grow in its native environment, where it will best support other life forms – insects, birds, animals, reptiles, fishes in pools and woodland herbs.

You can do this spell, with appropriate changes to the words, for any one particular species or for an area, such as a local wood or a hedgerow. It is obviously more effective to bless your local trees or a threatened species, since the spell will be less general and therefore less thinly spread.

If campaigning to save even one single tree from the developer's axe, you should try to speak the curse against abuse daily and not rely on saying it just once or twice. If said regularly the effect of a spell will be cumulative, and one very small spell will become something enormous. In such a case, you could bless the threatened tree or forest area with safety rather than with increase, as follows.

In the names of the Lady and Lord
of natural magic and the World Wood,
let this tree [or trees] of [name the area]
always be blessed
with absolute safety. Let none molest.
Let it be protected with harm to none
to live out all its natural life
and to reproduce, free from harm or strife.
By all the powers of wind, light,
rain, land and wraith.
and by three times three,
safety, safety, safety for this tree [these trees]
safety, safety, safety for this tree,
safety, safety, safety for this tree
for now and always.
So may this be.

Do not feel unsure of yourself when it comes to changing

my words for your purpose. Your spell does not have to rhyme. Simply speak from your heart about what you want and include the words 'with harm to none'. The power of a blessing derives from the following.

1 You wholeheartedly mean what you say and want it to happen without reservations.

2 You speak in the names of deities. (And these may be whomever you worship as Great Mother and All-Father and call upon either by names or just as 'Lady and Lord'.)

3 You invoke the help of elemental spirits, allying yourself with wind, light, rain, land and wraith

That's all there is to it. Easy, really. But do remember to make it conditional upon no one of any species (including yourself) being harmed in the process. Magic is an amoral and elemental thing, like electicity or a flowing river. It will always take the *easiest* route to achieve the stated objective unless *you* place boundaries around it and state that no one must be harmed.

Many New Age practices are not conditional at all, and, as a witch, this makes me uneasy. People just visualize what they want or 'order it up' from life and quite often there are no terms of kindliness concerning how their dreams might come true. It is just assumed there will be no casualties. But it doesn't necessarily work like that. And just because something is not called witchcraft but has some kind of non-threatening name, something without a dark glint or an edge of any kind, it doesn't mean that it can't be dangerous. It is still magic, but not always done with the expertise that a witch would hopefully, if properly taught, bring to the matter.

To return to our magical sequence, the example of a hedgerow rite, give to the tree you are actually touching or visualizing a well-wishing. Simply say, 'Tree, may you have long life and health and happiness' or something similar. Then ask the tree spirit to bless you in turn. Follow this with the tree-breathing exercise described in Chapter 2 (page 31). (And if you only have time for one hedgerow spell in a busy day and cannot possibly do this whole sequence, then the tree-breathing one is what I recommend).

As you end a session of spell-casting, it is important to ensure that you will be safe from psychic harm as you go about your daily life. I include below a spell for this.

Yes, I know. We are told to believe that while you are doing magical work, you might be attacked by evil spirits but that in normal daily life you are perfectly safe. Within mainstream culture, this is the message and many a horror film makes the point that it is by practising magic, or coming within the orbit of those who do, that you expose yourself to psychic attack. However, as any witch or psychic knows well, there are many places and situations in everyday life in which we can meet with aggressive, malicious or vampiric spirits. These may merely cause a shiver of unease but they *can* bring psychic disturbance in ourselves, leading to illness or a run of bad luck. Examples of such places are underground tube stations or haunted houses in which there have been acts of cruelty, murder, physical violence or any extreme form of abuse.

Some magical healers specialize in restoring the balance and lost harmony in such places. This is important work and very challenging indeed. However, those of us whose special skills and interests do not lie in such situations are better off leaving them. No witch can do everything, be all-powerful.

Anyway, all of us need to practise some form of psychic protection, to go safely through our lives, everywhere, whether spell-casting in a hedgerow or surfing the net in an office or library.

There are many, many ways to achieve psychic safety. Whole books have been written about this one subject, alone. So this last spell in the hedgerow rite is just one way of going about it though it *is* an old method, tried and tested.

You need to carry a holly leaf in your pocket or in a pouch or bag, perhaps hanging from your belt. And to say this.

Spell for Psychic Protection

Powers of the boundary, keep me from harm.
Keep me in safety by this strong charm.
Presence of holly, bright spirit power,
keep me in safety, each minute and hour.
By root and stem, leaf, fruit and flower,
through day and night, in dark or light,
everywhere, protect me.
So may it be.

Part of the strength of this spell is derived from its invocation of wholeness, which is achieved by naming each part of a plant ('By root and stem' etc.). Such an invocation, in magical thought, is a way of attaining an aura of completeness and therefore power, around yourself.

Holly is said to be one of the strongest of all plants when it comes to psychic protection. If you choose a leaf from a female tree it will have fewer prickles and be more comfortable to carry. It is frequently found in hedgerows as well as in woods and gardens. Other hedgerow plants credited with being psychically protective are hawthorn,

blackthorn and blackberry. If you live far from these kind of plants, you could carry birch or rowan. Change the words of the spell to suit the tree or herb. In a land where none of these is found growing, you might choose acacia, aloe vera, anise, bamboo, cactus, carob, dogwood, eucalyptus, garlic, huckleberry, lilac, oak, papaya, peony, pepper tree, sandalwood, willow, witch hazel or yerba santa. Powerful psychic protectors are found in all parts of the world.

Having asserted your psychic safety, you are now ready to return to the everyday world. Say something like this.

I give thanks to all the elemental spirits
of wind, light, rain, land and wraith
for their blessing. Hail and farewell.

I give thanks also to all the spirits
of tree and boundary and forest
who have assisted me. Hail and farewell.

I give thanks to the Lady and Lord
of natural magic and the World Wood
for all their blessings upon us all
and upon my life and work.
And I ask their blessing now
as I depart from the hedgerow [boundary].

If indoors, return now to the place between two staffs or twigs in which you began the rite. But face in the opposite direction – away from your altar and working area. If outside, return to the hedge/boundary/woodland edge facing away from the forest/sea/place beyond the hedge where you have just been. Conclude the rite with words that state your intention to return to the everyday world. For example, you might say the following.

I now return to the human community.
May I walk my path there as a hedge witch
in love and wisdom, health and happiness
and in prosperity. May my psychic senses return
to a state suitable for the mundane, the world
of thought, talk and practicality.

Then step away from the edge or boundary.

The foregoing rite is an example of hedge witchcraft. It is not the only possible interpretation of this ancient theme. The work is adaptable, endlessly changing to meet the demands of differing times and circumstances. It is creative and always has been throughout the ages. Though deeply spiritual, it is much more like an artform than a religion. There is no dogma and, as with oil painting or theatre, no definitive version exists. Instead, any version is true if it works for you as an interpretation of the tradition and yields results. Therefore, you do not have to learn all these lengthy spells unless you want to. I have given them, in full like this, the better to convey the ideas and principles. It is up to you whether to use them or to use only your own words, either planned or spontaneous. However, if you are new to all this, I do advise you to study my examples carefully and to try them out.

Read through the above rite once or twice, imagining the hedgerow, the plants you might work with, the feel of a tree trunk against your hands as you give a blessing or practise tree-breathing. Next, you might practise the tree-breathing exercise outside with an actual tree, perhaps in your garden. When you are ready, read the whole sequence formally, either before an indoor altar or outside in a real hedge or forest edge. See how this feels. Do you now want to memorize the words or to say words of your own?

It is perfectly possible to be a hedge witch with remark-ably little use of spoken spells, utilizing your communion with tree and elemental spirits, the power of herbs, ritual gestures, visualization and strong clarity about your inten-tions. For myself, since enchantment is my special skill, I find that word-magic is the essential thread upon which all else is strung. But there are other ways and I firmly believe that a willingness just to go out on the land and sense the presence of tree spirits, elemental powers, elves and the Earth herself is the basis of all the rest. However we dress it up or down, the work of the hedge sitter is to be in communion with spirit presences, in alliance with them, within the natural world, on behalf of humanity. *To make of the boundary a place of union.*

Chapter 5

Elves and the World Tree

The hedge witch of pre-Christian Northern Europe, in common with other magical practitioners of the time, had a world view that was based on unity. In this cosmology, it was understood that every aspect of creation was connected with all else. Thus, you could not affect one person, creature, plant or place without beginning a chain of events that affected, in however small a way, all others, everywhere. All acts and spells were known to have far-reaching implications because of this. For example, one person's kind deed for a stranger could lower the second person's stress to such an extent that it averted the row they would have had with a family member, so saving a third person from an accident they would otherwise have had because upset. Not having an accident could mean that they remained an efficient worker, so saving their children from going hungry that winter – and so on.

These chains of cause and effect, which could be creative or destructive, were not seen as limited only to human relationships. All plants and creatures and every kind of elf or sprite were also a part of this continuum, known as 'the web of wyrd'.

By the same token, we were seen as living our lives as a result of the acts and decisions of others, both human and non-human, rather than solely because of our own choices. Elemental spirits and land-elves, as well as the men and women who worked in the fields, put food on our tables. For a start, elemental spirits kept the winds blowing, the waters flowing, the crops growing. Other people's ancestors as well as our own created a culture in which we could each thrive and, hopefully, survive. In effect, no deed was ever done single-handedly.

Recognizing this, the hedge witch made many psychic links with helpful spirits and also worked for a good alignment with all aspects of creation. In this chapter we will look at what this means and how to do it.

As hedge witches, we base our work on the knowledge that we are each a co-creator of life and reality. And that this is as true for those who work magic as it is in the rational, practical realm. However, magical skill means more power so we need to be specially careful that our spells serve life for the good of us all. In doing that, we will attract round us many benign spirit presences, just as a person undertaking a practical, creative project will always attract like-minded friends. No one ever wields real power all by themselves. A hedge witch, however solitary, however reclusive, will have the assistance of many spirits because our work has an impact on the spirit realms. Such magical power as we possess is always a collective matter.

In Pagan tradition in Northern Europe (and in other cultures as well) there was a symbol for what stood at the centre of the whole web of life. This was the World Tree, a cosmic axis. It linked all beings all around, and those above and below as well. Within this model, life was seen as having, basically, three dimensions.

First, there was that around the tree trunk and among its lower branches. This was known as Middle Earth and comprised the whole of the natural world in its living glory and physicality. It is, of course, the dimension in which we as humans, live out our lives. But it is not just concrete reality. This is the realm of the natural magic inherent in herbs, pools, places, birds, animals, crystals and also the land-elves, who dwell in its subtle psychic aspect.

The word 'elves' by the way was a catch-all term denoting 'spirits' to some of our ancestors. There are many types of elf (or faerie, if you prefer that term). As hedge witches, we work with some of them and, in fact, are often taught by them as well as assisted in our magic. This is traditional for a witch, as many attested in former centuries. I, myself, have often been taught – through psychic communication – by a wise faerie teacher. I work with faerie familiars, constantly.

In addition (and in common with a number of other witches) I also believe myself to be part faerie. To believe oneself to have faerie blood or to have a fay spirit in a human body was not unusual in past centuries. That is because elves, faeries, live solid, corporeal lives in their own parallel dimension (a place known in myth as 'the Otherworld'). Tales of travelling back and forth between the worlds were not uncommon. They are not unknown now. As I said, I have done it myself. Therefore, relationships between humans and those of faerie kind could exist and are said, in folklore, to have produced children. That is how present-day people can claim to have faerie blood.

If all this sounds too far-fetched for your taste, too fantastical, treat it all as, well, a faerietale. One that can yield a poetic truth and bring inspiration. Your spells will be just as effective whether or not you take this kind of thing literally. Meanwhile, it's important to acknowledge that our ancestors *did* take it all seriously. We can create rites of hedge witchcraft that are well founded in folklore and tradition by involving ourselves with the elves. For such purposes, they are indeed spirits, since our connection with them is mainly psychic rather than physical.

As I said, around the World Tree there is the realm called Middle Earth, the domain of the land-elves. Under the Tree, beneath its roots, there is a place called the Underworld. This, partly, is the realm of the dead and therefore of those awaiting rebirth. (Our Pagan ancestors believed in rebirth, as do most hedge witches today. If you do not, then it is fine to treat the idea as a symbol for how life goes on, after each loss or death.)

Another kind of elf lives down there. These are called dark-elves. In spite of their name, which may sound threatening, these are not evil baddies but psychic alchemists who can make jewellery from rough ore, compost from corruption, new psychic skills from the psychic dismemberment experienced in some mental illnesses. The dead spend some of their time between lives within the realm of the dark-elves. But the elves themselves are not usually dead. (Elves are not immortal but live much longer than humans.) The dark-elves simply live in the Underworld, among the dead while themselves living.

Here, I must say that Pagans do not believe that bad people go to the Underworld, while the good go to heaven. All the dead go to the Underworld first, as it is a place of purification where our cares and sorrows are stripped from us and important psychic 'processing' happens. It is a place of great beauty. Afterwards, we go to the Upperworld, where rest and inspiration occur, in preparation for the next life. (This is a very simple version. Northern European beliefs about the afterlife could be quite complex, involving nine different locations within the Underworld alone. Suffice it to say that all realms were seen as necessary aspects of creation.)

Those beings known as the dark-elves in Scandinavian and Germanic tradition had other names in other places. To the Brythonic Celts, they were the people of Annwn, an Otherworld paradise where old age and sickness do not exist. They were also known as the fay of Avalon. 'The people of the hill' was another popular title, referring to elves who served Mother Holle or Hel, the Underworld goddess. To the Irish, they are the people of Tir Nan Og. The Abapansi are faeries known to the Amazulu tribe of Africa and they lead people beyond death into the Otherworld.

Dark-elves are found under all lands on Earth (in a parallel dimension) but differing cultures perceive them in various ways. To the Nordic people, they were small and dark, akin to dwarves. The Irish saw them as tall and beautiful, whether dark or fair in colouring, and noble in bearing. (Actually, those from the Underworld are of a great many types and races.)

Whatever their kind, their realm is the one in which transmutation takes place – and that's all we need to know for our purposes as hedge witches. They can be asked to bless all magic that aims to change corruption into the nourishment for good new growth. They make 'psychic compost'.

As dwarves, the dark-elves are said to be supreme in transmuting rough ore and uncut crystals into fine jewellery and other artefacts. The fay of the Underworld are all craftspeople, artists, musicians or poets, whether we call them dwarves or by some other name. Theirs are the spells by which loss and conflict can be transformed into new understanding, artwork, wisdom, a powerful story – something to enhance life.

Down in the Underworld, there are also spirits of the processes by which dead plants and the bodies of creatures are transformed into new nourishment for fresh growth. This, too, has the dark-elves' blessing.

If you have difficulty believing in elves as literal presences, with an objective life of their own, that is not a problem. Many a witch decides that all faeries are really personifications of certain life processes, poetic metaphors for, say, the spirits of transformation or just of magic. Myself, I believe in them literally but I know that they have symbolic meaning as well, It is up to you to decide what you think as there is no dogma in hedge witchcraft.

Dark-elves and their realm have been demonized, as though the processes of change in death were something unhealthy or even evil. Thus, the *swart-alfa* or, as in Scotland, the *unseelie* court of dark faeries were often believed to be bad spirits. There are mischief-makers and corrupt characters amongst all types of elves (just as there are amongst human beings and other species). But a dualistic division of realms or of types of elves into 'good' and 'evil' does not tend to be the rule in Pagan spirituality.

Above, among the top branches of the World Tree, is the realm of the light-elves. Here, dwell the beings that many now call angels. However, they are not necessarily connected with Christianity or Judaism. They were known in many indigenous, pre-Christian cultures in all parts of the world. They are sometimes called the Shining Ones. Their bodies are of intensely coloured light. They often appear as tall women or men with robes of white, crimson, emerald or blue. They can also be silver or gold or combinations of colours. They do not always have wings like the classic angel but have a billowing aura of light around them that may look like wings. Sometimes they appear as abstract shapes of light. They are seen in wild places like woodlands and on the sea shore as well as on hilltops. They bring a sense of exhilaration. Like all the elves, they are wild and free, as unfettered as the wind and as unassailable as a rainbow – with the same kind of remote beauty that can't be used nor ever possessed.

Light-elves often help us but they are not (as in today's popular conception) permanent personal assistants with wings and powers. Most of the light-elves mind elven business. They are not so concerned with human desires as we may sometimes like to think. Instead, they take a much broader view, being concerned with the welfare of all species, a greater harmony, and with their own projects and existence. Light-elves remind us that existence is a great joy. The point of life is simply to live, celebrating creative evolution by dancing to harmony. I have seen them dancing the world towards greater balance, simply from happiness.

The presence of light-elves has also been noted in many places on Earth besides Northern Europe. Australian Aboriginal people have seen them and so have Japanese Shintoists. However, they do not much like cities and are said to find traffic fumes and any airborne pollution hard to cope with. This is one reason why they may not be seen so often as in former centuries. Yet they still contact people psychically, so are still able to help and guide even when not in our vicinity. They offer this help when our purposes align with theirs as bringers of harmony. In no sense are they psychic nannies prepared to grant all human wishes.

The same thing goes for dark-elves and land-elves, too. Their aims may seem inscrutable to an everyday human mind. They care about the natural world and they also care for natural justice. They revel in freedom, song and dance, love, celebration and adventure. They are not keen on concepts of cold duty or self-denial. They don't like self-pity. They think human behaviour is more or less insane much of the time – and dangerous. They watch, warily.

Light-elves are specialists in vision. They can help us to see the way forward, even in very hard circumstances. Sometimes, they will bestow upon us a guiding vision which may appear when we close our eyes in meditation or simply as a 'daydream'. Whether we think they're objectively real or that they're personifications of some visionary aspect of our own psychology, they can help us gain inspiration and hope and a broader outlook.

In Northern European mythology, the light-elves' realm is said to consist of beautiful forests where all plants and creatures live happily. They are said to be under the care of 'the Lord', Freyr, the Norse god of nature. He is the equivalent of the horned green god of natural balance and natural justice worshipped by many of today's Pagans. Indeed, he may be the origin of today's ideas about 'the Green Man', a forest god who protects the environment. He is usually worshipped together with the goddess of natural magic in realms here, below and above, She is sometimes known as 'the Lady', Freya.

We might say that the light-elves and also the deities associated with them (who are known by many names, worldwide) imply an ideal state. They may be guardians of our images of a pre-Fall innocence in which all beings live in true harmony. The image of the *belle sauvage* or noble savage belongs to this realm as does every dream and practice of oneness with nature that has inspired indigenous people and today's environmentalists. This is a good and necessary dream, in view of the cost to the biosphere when we fail, collectively, to live lightly on the Earth.

I haven't yet said much about the land-elves, those who

live in the subtle, psychic dimension of our own world. That is because they are more easily understood by most people than are the dark-elves or light-elves. They are often referred to as nature spirits. They are known in every culture on Earth, so far as I know. In Eastern Europe, they are the *vila*, who look after the health of orchard and garden, field and woodland. The *aguane* and *silvani* of Italy protect streams, mountains and forests. In Switzerland, the land-elves are called *erdluitle*. They protect the natural world and also increase the harvest by dancing in farmland. In New Zealand, there are Maori faeries called the *patu-paiarehe*. They live in trees and bushes. The *kachina* are elves known to the Hopi and Pueblo peoples of North America. They live within and work with the forces of nature.

Wherever they are, the elves of the Earth can take various forms. They can be very small, or large as giants, and may appear as creatures or in a more or less human form or as something between human and creature. For example, they may be women with hooves instead of feet. They live in the natural features of any landscape.

So much for the three elven realms we could call 'here, below and above'. In the most complex form of Northern European mythology there are subsections within each of them but this need not concern us as hedge witches. For all practical purposes, we can make magic with ease by connecting with the three and with their inhabitants. Above all, we need to remember that each one has links with the others. As hedge witches, we can understand this universal integration of the three realms by looking at any tree in a garden or park or hedgerow or forest. This is because *any* tree has all the qualities of the World Tree within itself. It has roots under the land, in the realm underneath all surface appearances. It has branches reaching up to the light. And it grows right here in Middle

Earth, supporting and being supported by many insects, birds, creatures and elementals.

Hedge witches can ride the World Tree, travelling up and down its trunk in many ways to reach the various realms. And there are many ways in which this theme of the World Tree can be central to us in magical rites. In the rite that follows, we shall connect with the elves, to cast a powerful spell of initiation as a hedge witch. Its purpose is to help us to make strong links with elven realms and so to stand in alignment with elven spirits in magical work. This increases our magical strength while dedicating it to healing purposes.

Rite of the World Tree

Dress in mismatched clothing, as is traditional for a hedge witch – for example wear odd socks or shoes with odd laces. Add any other items of witch wear that you may have acquired. This need not include a black cloak or pointy hat unless you want it to. (It is more likely that our ancestors in England wore a red hat while working magic. There are many references in folklore and legend to the 'red cap' worn by a wise woman.) While we are on the subject, you may also want to wear a belt from which you can hang a pouch of cloth or leather. In such a receptacle, wise women and cunning men of the past carried items to do with their spells, things like psychically protective slivers of wood, holed stones for healing talismans or chips of amber for increased magical power or for prosperity. Nowadays, these bags are of any colour the user deems appropriate. For example, they may be of green if the emphasis is upon physical well-being and prosperity or black if there is a desire to keep some item protected from psychic harm. Red is a good all-purpose colour and strongly linked with faerie.

Begin by standing in a hedgerow or at a forest edge between trees. If you are working indoors, stand between two staffs, or even two sticks or twigs, in a symbolic hedgerow. Place your non-dominant foot forward.

Begin with a hedgerow spell for altered consciouness, such as the one on page 51.

It is usual when practising magic to define a sacred dimension to the place where you are working and also to call upon guardian spirits to protect you psychically. Here, a very simple invocation of elves and the powers of spirit friendship takes the place of more formal methods. Walk forward three paces and pause. Say the following.

I walk forward to become the friend
of healing spirits of every kind,
Below, above and in Middle Earth.
By all the powers in the World Wood,
in the names of the Greenwood Lady and Lord,
friendship keep me from all unrest
that no bad spirit may me molest.
The friendship of elves keep me from harm
as my heart is friendly. This is the charm.
I call upon elves by Mother Earth blessed.
Hail! Hail and welcome!

Pause to speak – in your mind or out loud – to any spirit presences whom you may see or sense as a result of your call to them. There may be dwarves, light-elves, land-elves, human ancestral spirits or ghostly creatures. If you sense nothing and no one, this may be because they are biding their time before becoming tangible – perhaps watching you from a small distance. Some friendships cannot be rushed.

A hedge witch has always worked with spirit allies, known as 'familiars'. The word 'familiar' means 'friend'. Spirit friends assist us with magic and so our links with them, which are psychic, are extremely important to us.

As ever, I advise you to ignore the question of whether or not elves really exist. If you do not believe in them, you can see this rite as a way of relating to aspects of yourself and the natural world. It can work just as well that way because our work is transpersonal, a matter of our own inner selves *and* our relationship with the soul of nature, the life force.

Add the following.

Greenwood Lady and Lord of natural magic
in all worlds, here, below and above,
powers of beauty and truth and love,
watch over me and bless this rite
in this realm, in the depths, in the height.
I invoke you by this sign.

Raise your wand or staff in the air and use it to draw the stylized shape of a heart. If you don't yet have either of these, use your forefinger instead. The heart is an obvious symbol of love and also, in Northern European tradition, a symbol of Mother Earth herself. For our ancestors, Earth was invoked together with her daughters and sons, the elves, and deities connected with faerie, on especially solemn and sacred occasions.

Now walk forward to a tree that is healthy and full grown, not a sapling. If working in winter, try to choose one of an evergreen species. (A yew is ideal.) If indoors, walk forward to a staff that is propped so that it is upright, to represent the World Tree, the cosmic axis. At the base, there should be a small pot of earth that stands in for the land from which the tree grows. (Outdoors, of course, you will not need the pot of earth.) Place your hand upon the tree or staff and say:

Tree of [name the species], may you be to me
as the World Tree, itself
for all the purposes of this rite.
With your help may I now be aligned
with healing dark-elves, land-elves
and elves of the light.
You are at the centre, in harmony
with the whole web of wyrd, web of destiny,
that links us all, each to each.
In all my work as a hedge witch
it is my will to be at one
with this and with the will of the elves
who sew joy, health, freedom and natural justice,
stitch by magical stitch.

Dig a small hole in the ground or in your pot of earth and then say this:

I now turn to the realm below, the dimension under the roots of the World Tree.
Dark-elves you dwellers in underground halls, you who trans-form pain and loss and corruption into the raw materials for new life, you who take dross and change it by magical artistry into bright beauty, I call upon you, I invoke you, by this place of burial which I have newly dug.

Indicate the hole you have made. Then say:

And I place within the burial pit all that I must give up or which must be changed for my life as a hedge witch to flourish in wisdom and magical strength. I place herein self-destructive behaviour, wrong attitudes and unhealthy addictions. Yours is the realm of necessity, whereby we can grow in inner beauty. So let it be with me. And let these necessary changes happen without harm to anyone. Befriend and assist me now, dark-elves, and help me from now on with all my spells.

Place within the hole some clippings from your own finger or toe nails. (Yes, I know, that sounds bizarre but it is common practice among witches to use either hair or nails as a representative of the whole person from whom they came, when casting spells. As we now know, each smallest part contains the DNA of the entire body so this old tradition is not so far from being reasonable.) Say:

As these nails are given to the ground
to become one with nature's round
may all that is mine now be aligned
with the magical will of elven kind
to restore harmony and wild joy
in every realm, in life unbound.

Cover the nails with earth, to bury them. If you are working indoors, put them in the earth in the pot and then bury the contents outside after you've finished the rite.

Next, stand and look up through the branches of the tree towards the sky. (If indoors, look up and then close your eyes, picturing the sky instead.) Say something like this:

I look up to the realm above. Among the branches of the World Tree are sources of light, by which we see. Light-elves, you who have bodies of air and fire and wraith and are everywhere, our guiding visions to bless and to give, bless the bright dreams by which I live.

Hold up to them a skein of rainbow threads. These can be embroidery cotton, wool or any (preferably natural) fibre.

The threads should be of equal length and about one handspan long. Lay them together and then tie a knot in the whole bundle to keep them from falling apart or tangling. Say:

Light-elves, I offer to you my dream of myself as a hedge witch, as I raise these threads. Bless my dream, may it serve us all, whether elven, creaturely, plant or elemental.

Now describe your personal vision of what it may mean to you, ideally, to be a hedge witch. For example, say something like this:

Here is my dream. I'm a spirit traveller, wand wielder, broomstick bestrider, I'm a hedge rider. I'm a wise woman/cunning man, a magical healer and an enchantress/enchanter, a mistress/master of spells.

I am on a quest for magical wisdom. I seek to blend my every spell with the greater magic of evolution, which is in the hands of the fates, the wyrd sisters, the keepers of balance in all dimensions throughout the web of wyrd, web of destiny. Let my quest lead to wisdom and power in equal measure. This is my dream.

May I do no harm but help to heal the life of any for whom I bespell, whether that be person, plant, creature, place, elemental spirit or elf. May I be at one with your realm of guiding visions of beauty. Befriend me, light-elves. Bless and watch over me.

Conclude by touching the rainbow threads to the ground or, if indoors, to the earth in the pot. Thus, you have made a symbolic link, a 'rainbow bridge' between the realm of guiding visions and that of earthly life. From now on the threads should be kept in a safe place or carried with you in your 'charm bag' – the pouch that hangs from your belt.

Stand facing the tree trunk. Say something like this:

I turn to the realm which is all around
below the sky and above the ground,
around the trunk of the great World Tree.
Here, in the world of material beauty,
I call to you now, the elves of the land
who care for the living balance of nature.
As I honour Mother Earth and her children,
the Greenwood Lady and Lord, take my hand.

Extend your hand in a symbolic gesture of friendship with land-elves. Say something like this:

In my life as a hedge witch, may I bring blessings of health, good
fortune and abundance to plants and creatures and to wild
natural places, as well as to humans. So may I be aligned with
your purposes, healing land-elves, throughout the Earth, at one
with you in your magical work.
   As I bless, so may I be blessed. I bring you this gift.

Pour out milk or cream on the ground in offering. Let it seep right in. If indoors, pour it out into the pot of earth, the contents of which will be buried outside later on. Say:

> *This is an offering to you, land-elves. May you be blessed, too, with health, good fortune and prosperity. May I be accepted as your friend. I ask that you befriend me. Blessed be.*

Stand with your back to the tree or staff for a while, contemplating the three realms of existence – below, above and here. Understand, that they are not really separate from each other but are dimensions of the one reality, which contains us all and of which we are part.

Gradually, in your imagination, let yourself become one with the World Tree by blending with the tree beside you (or with an imagined tree, if working indoors). This is done in the following way.

Becoming One with the World Tree

Close your eyes and imagine yourself becoming less solid. Your flesh and bones are gradually ceasing to be firm and earthy. You are becoming your own ghost-presence, your spirit body – which is there all the time in reality but of which you are normally unconscious. Imagine you are looking down at your own legs and feet and the ground upon which you stand. Do not picture yourself as a figure on a screen looking at the ground. Instead, *be* the person looking down at your feet and then up at elven reality. In your imagination, inhabit your body from within – as usual. If you treat yourself as an object to be observed from a detached vantage, you will not do this kind of psychic work successfully. (However, it is a mistake quite often made by apprentice witches). In this form, you can pass through walls or rock faces or into the trunks of trees.

Now ask the actual tree you are working with – whether this is a physical being or an imagined one – if you can be at one with it, in union. Ask this silently, inside your mind. Sense the answer. If it is 'yes', imagine you slip inside the tree trunk, becoming one with it and with the entire tree. Change your shape, in imagination, projecting yourself to the topmost branches and into the leaves and down the trunk to roots below ground. Sense the tree's own sense of itself and of its reality through the seasons. After a while, you may transcend any sense of yourself as a separate being and so experience a union with all creation around the tree.

This is a joyful experience, even ecstatic, and it will increase your awareness of spirit presences in your life generally. It can also bring a strong surge of magical power which may at once be channelled into a spontaneous spell for healing. You may only achieve the necessary self-transcendence for a few brief moments. But, in a sense, this state is timeless (or is an example of time in faerie realms which is known to run differently from ours). A few moments may be all you need.

If you don't succeed with this exercise, don't despair. It is much easier if you don't try too hard. An approach that is relaxed and playful and open-minded about results is more likely to get you somewhere. And where it gets you may not be what I have described and experienced. You may discover some other state or way that is equally valid and empowering. This kind of work can only be done in a spirit of adventure and exploration and it is an art, not a technology.

You may, when experienced, take psychic journeys to any one of the three elven realms in this way. Using imagination as the great key to faerie realms, you may commune psychically with spirit presences who are not part of imagination but exist in their own right. These may bring you insights and prophecies and give assistance with spells – if they approve of your aims.

Finally, in imagination, separate out from the tree and regain your human form. Let your body become solid. Thank the tree, adding:

> *Tree, you stand at the centre of the whole web of life, in which shining threads of spirit link each being to all else. May you be blessed for your part in life and in this rite. May there be an increase of your living species. May your kind increase in numbers, in harmony with all other species.*

Pause and then continue:

> *I thank you also, dark-elves, light-elves and land-elves, for help and blessing.*
>
> *And I thank you, Lady and Lord of the Greenwood, Goddess and God of natural magic, for watching over me. As I return to the realm of humanity, may I remain at one with your healing purposes. Hail and farewell.*

Return to the hedge or forest edge (or stand between your two staffs). Cast your hedgerow spell for psychic protection (page 73).

Conclude the rite with the words, 'May my psychic senses now return to a state suitable for everyday life in the human world.'

As with any rite or any kind of psychic work, you should now allow a gradual period of readjustment to mundane life. It is not wise to drive, operate machinery or walk in any dangerous place (such as a cliff path) until you are certain that you are fully restored to rational consciousness. This may take anything from a few minutes to a few hours, according to your temperament and type but only you can be the judge. In the intervening time, you can go for a gentle walk or sit somewhere for a drink or some food. Or you can simply rest. It is up to you.

As this rite demonstrates, it is the dark-elves who hold the secrets of success in magic. Genuine witchcraft is not done only by directing goodwill and healing power at any problem. That is because we need to deal with the causes of any conflict, illness or lack or happiness – to clean up first and so to transmute them. Otherwise, it is like trying to paint a beautiful picture on top of an ugly one, without first returning the canvas to a neutral, background shade, or like bringing new furniture into a filthy room, or like planting vegetables in land that is undug and unfertilized.

Transforming the tangled threads of our old problems into a kind of psychic compost is the work of the dark-elves and nothing new can be built up successfully without their help.

I stress this point because humankind tends to fear the dark-elves and their realm, preferring the equally important but more obviously likeable light-elves. I think it may be our acceptance of spirit realms below that distinguishes a witch from other kinds of spirit healer. We know that goodwill and blessings are not always enough, important though they are.

In the Pagan world of the past, many offerings were made to the elves/faeries by our ancestors and so when we hedge witches give things to the elves in our rites we are recreating a very old tradition. The ancestors gave things to gain faerie blessing upon crops in field and orchard and upon livestock. Their gifts were known in Northern Europe as an 'elf-blot' and often included meat or blood. Other common gifts were milk, cream, honey or cakes and grain. The elves are said to take the spirit essence of what is given to them, leaving just the material form of the milk, honey etc.

Strengthened by gifts, the elves can work much more effectively within our realm, from which the gifts came. By giving such things as food or drink or water in which to wash or even garlands of flowers and precious stones, we are offering hospitality to spirits, making a place for them in our realm. (I believe the same idea is current in some places in Asia, where little wooden houses are made for the spirits to dwell in.) This makes them stronger in our reality than they would otherwise have been and also creates a friendliness between humans and elves, to the benefit of each.

Remember, the elves are not 'somewhere else'. All types of elves, whether of the dark, light or land, are actually right here on this Earth, but in more subtle dimensions. Therefore, co-operation is in the interests of all beings. We must welcome the elves.

If you find all this a touch fanciful remember also that many tribal cultures throughout the world have believed in the elves (by whatever name they knew them). When the woods and wells, hilltops and beaches are said to be the haunts of faeries, strong psychic bonds are experienced between humankind and the environment. This is because the land is seen as numinous, a place of mystery, and so *sacred*. Whatever you actually believe, giving simple gifts to local spirits benefits the subtle dimensions of human culture and the ways in which we experience nature. It is a strongly creative act.

In the past, the practice of offering things to the elves reminded people at the very least that we live within nature spiritually as well as physically. That we are not apart from nature but a part of her, along with trees, animals and everything else. And also that we must live in a balance that includes giving as well as taking.

As a hedge witch however, I know that the elves who tend the natural world – in all its many aspects and dimensions – make powerful, fair-minded friends.

Chapter 6

Broomsticks and Staffs

A hedge witch's role might be defined as 'go–between'. You go between the human community and spirit realms for magical purposes. Sometimes, however, you go to give magical help, such as a blessing for trees or creatures, within the Otherworld. That is, you may walk right into faerie, physically, and do some magical work there. Much more often, you give blessings within the 'dreamscape', the psychic dimension, the place where human imagination and elven activity intersect. After all, that is the hedge witch's real territory.

To work for trees in the Otherworld or the realm between worlds affects our own trees as well as those in faerie forests. That is because the land-elves and all elves live in subtle dimensions of this same Earth which we inhabit. I am not saying here that there are no elves on other planets or in other universes. For all that I know, there are many of them. But for all practical purposes, elves that we meet are here on this Earth with us. And all their realms are subtle dimensions of the same universe in which we live.

Sometimes, we go 'between the worlds' to gain information about what the elves may require of us to maintain our friendship with them or to divine what is needed to cast any particular spell. Or we may simply go exploring or go to develop magical skills.

To go 'between the worlds' is to travel in spirit, in most instances. Your body does not normally leave Middle Earth. But there have been cases, such as the famous one of Thomas the Rhymer, a thirteenth-century Scot, in which a physical journey was undertaken right into the faerie dimension of Earth, the Otherworld. Sometimes, faeries have come to live here, in the everyday human reality. The tale of the 'green children' who wandered into a medieval Suffolk village is thought to be one such case and folklore recounts many, many others. You can walk physically into an area of the Otherworld but it is rare and not without risk to do that. You may find the portal back to your own time and place has closed behind you. Or you may get back quite easily, only to find that weeks, months, years, even hundreds of years have passed in the human world since you were gone. That is because time runs differently there.

As hedge witches, we practise spirit travelling when we go between the worlds to another realm. Our bodies stay safely in this human world while, in a state like a dream in which we are fully conscious, our spirits 'ride the broomstick' to other places. We are hedge riders as well as hedge sitters, flying in spirit by means of plants. We ride the hedge by bestriding a staff or broom. This seems to be an ancient technique.

In tribal cultures throughout Europe and on other continents the wooden staff has always been seen as a magical tool and connected with travelling. All practitioners of magic, whether calling themselves shaman, wise woman, cunning man, witch, hedge priest or priestess, Druid, wizard or anything else were likely to have one.

The Scandinavian Bronze Age priestesses of Freya are

believed to have had wooden staffs. Indeed, to be a staff-bearing woman was once considered a public sign of dedication to this most magical of all the Northern goddesses. Since Freya and her brother Freyr are very like the Lady and Lord worshipped by today's Wiccans (witches in covens), we can see that the use of a staff – disguised in more recent centuries as a broomstick – has ancient roots in more ways than one.

The staff of a priestess had many functions. It could cast a spell by being used to touch somebody, or trees, or creatures, or any object or place or building. The type of spell would depend upon the intention of the staff bearer and the words said by her. At other times, the staff could be used to pound the earth, rhythmically, as a means of calling on such spirits as were believed to be under the ground. These could be ancestral spirits who were consulted about the tribe's welfare, or they could be nature spirits of underground wells or seams of minerals, or they could be dark-elves whose help was sought for a number of reasons. The pounding might also be a call to land-elves or place spirits overseeing the health of crops, forests or animal species. Natural magicians have always knocked on the land's door, as it were, to gain admission to psychic realms and achieve psychic communion with spirit presences.

This practice isn't precisely flying upon a staff to the land of the elves but it is one way to bring communication with them by using one.

In many Pagan communities of the past, in many lands, the village women rode brooms or poles in the fields in the springtime, cantering round on them. They jumped as high as they could while astride. This was intended as sympathetic magic to bring a good harvest. In other words, the crops were supposed to grow as high as the brooms or poles 'flew'.

Brian Bates, in his book *The Real Middle Earth*, tells us that Anglo-Saxon wizards would use a staff to draw a circle upon the ground, in which to draw up and contain power from the land the better to work magic. He also tells us that in many cultures, a staff represents both the World Tree – the symbolic cosmic axis linking the world's various dimensions – *and* the ability of the bearer to travel in spirit. It implied spirit flight. Thus, a staff not only directs power from or to the bearer but also helps to convey the bearer's spirit from place to place.

Spirit travelling, as a practice inherited by today's witches, really is extremely important. After all, the image of a flying witch on a broomstick almost defines us! By such means we can, for example, fly to the bedside of a sick friend, the better to chant a healing spell for them. Or we can visit trees, creatures or far-away places to banish harm from them or to bless them.

We can do all this by psychic means. That is to say, by entering a state of dreaming while awake. This is exactly like dreaming asleep, in so far as events we witness may happen spontaneously, of their own volition. There are elements of the practice known as creative visualization but spirit journeying is much more than that. We may decide what we want to see or do and conjure it, using imagination to do so. However we may meet nature spirits, elves or people who have died and these presences have their own ideas and are autonomous in their actions.

In the spirit realm, it is important to look out from our own eyes, as in waking life. It does not work if you merely *picture yourself* doing things in a spirit realm. Your consciousness must be transferred to your spirit self in the dreamscape, so that you see from that perspective, so that you are, as far as you are concerned, actually there and not merely watching or visualizing yourself, as though on a screen. You must identify yourself with the figure in faerie realms, your spirit body, so that you look out, if anything, from an imaginary hedge and back towards the human community. That is real spirit travelling or one metaphor for what it is like. Imagination is required to achieve the state but it can be easily done once you have had practice. The effect of the switch of perspective is magical and does result in an increased capacity for real psychic experience.

How can you make things up like that, in imagination, and yet meet with spirits whom you have not made up nor visualized within the same imagined scene? How can any spirit with an objectively real presence be 'inside your head'? A witch would say that it is because the inner world has no more boundaries than does the outer one where we live bodily. Within the everyday physical world, we all breathe the same air and our lives are lit and made possible by the same sun that shines on us all. Beneath all our feet is the same solid ground because it is continuous from the North to the South Pole, even under the sea. We share the same world, within and without, and many so-called boundaries are illusory. There is just one world, one consciousness. That is why telepathy is possible.

Perhaps I should not say that boundaries are an illusion. They're more a protection, a useful *convention*, psychically speaking. Most of us are born with lots of them built in to our budding minds. Psychic people can open or close them more or less at will but we all need them. We are all born in the psychic equivalent of one unfenced world. But we do construct – and inherit – some mental fences for our own good since otherwise we would all be overwhelmed by the amount of psychic information available to us. It would be rather like living with dozens of televisions and radios inside our heads and all tuned to a different channel. We would go mad.

Like drug users on a 'bad trip', people with mental health problems may have too few psychic boundaries. Often, they feel disturbed or terrified. They need more inner hedges or fences. If you are such a person or think that you may be one, then you should not experiment with spirit travelling until you feel more grounded. If you do undertake such work when mentally unwell, it is at your own risk and should not be done without supervision from someone experienced in these arts. This is not because you will be pounced upon by bad spirits or anything dramatic like that but because a fragile mental balance should not be asked to accommodate extra experience in psychic realms.

For anyone averagely rational, this spirit work is as safe as taking a stroll down the road – if more surprising. After all, using the methods which I shall describe, you will not lose consciousness. Therefore, if you see anything which appears to you to be threatening, you can if you like return at once to the everyday world. All you need do is to open your eyes. You can then ask the powers of love, beauty and truth to protect you, addressing them as 'Lady and Lord' or by whatever names you know them.

What else can you do if you meet a spirit who seems unfriendly? Point your imagined wand at it and then visualize a flow of blue light coming from the tip to form a sort of protective screen between you and whatever it is that troubles you. If this is insufficient, use your wand to draw down a column of imagined white light, right over the top of the troublesome spirit, enclosing it. Then call on the friendly elves and the deities to take the spirit away to wherever it needs to go to be in harmony with life and all other beings. This never fails.

As I have said, all spirit journeys arise from having an altered consciousness. That is, they require you to be in a light trance state. There are well-documented, traditional ways for a witch to achieve this. One such practice was, quite simply, to ride a broomstick along the road or across country (as a physical act, not an imagined one). This just meant walking with your staff or broom between your legs and your feet on the ground as though on a hobby horse. There is a passage in Margaret Murray's book *The God of the Witches* describing a witch family in Lorraine, France, going to an actual historical sabbat in 1589. (The material in the book is taken from witch trials and eyewitness accounts given at the time.) In this instance the son rode on a stick and his mother on a pitchfork while the father rode on an ox. She also tells us that witches from Ireland and England as well as France were recorded (in the witch trials instigated by the Christian Church) as riding to sabbats upon sticks, brooms, rakes or forks. Once the sabbat began, there were ritual dances that people did while astride their sticks. There is no doubt that the broomstick riding and then the dancing, with the rhythmic actions involved, did help to change the witches' consciousness.

Such stick riding was a latter-day version of the shamanic pole riding in sacred ritual dances in Pagan tribal communities. However, whereas in earlier times such poles were not disguised, witches working in the Christian era hid their magical staffs by adding, for instance, a bundle of twigs or a pair of prongs to make a broom or fork. In fact, Murray tells us, medieval pictures of witchcraft tended to show female witches on brooms and male ones on forks. The reason for this would have been that possession of a broom by a woman or a fork by a man would arouse no suspicion that the possessors were practising magic. Anyone might own such things. Most people did.

Often, the staff or broom would be greased with the witches' famous flying ointment, made with hallucinogenic herbs. This was effective if the rider intended to mount the broomstick naked. If not, the ointment could be applied to the wrists and forehead of the rider.

In his book *The Roots of Witchcraft*, Michael Harrison tells us that a shortened 'broomstick' carved to resemble a man's penis was sometimes used by female witches as a magical dildo. This was first greased with flying ointment. The combination of sexual excitement and hallucinogenic herbs produced many visions for the witch. Particular herbs brought sensations of flying. Sometimes, the witch believed herself to have flown away bodily and attended a physical sabbat by this means.

Herbs and other substances that brought on visions were used throughout Pagan Europe, though not necessarily in combination with sexual practices, by male practitioners as well as female ones. We no longer know what quantities our ancestors may have used nor under what conditions. Surviving recipes for things like flying ointments tend to be incomplete. They do not state quantities, just ingredients. These include *Amanita muscaria*, the poisonous fungus known as fly agaric, as well as aconite, belladonna and hemlock. Aconite is highly toxic. Even to handle it without wearing gloves can lead to temporary paralysis. If ingested, it can cause permanent paralysis – or death. Belladonna is lethal in quite small doses. All parts of it contain atropine, a deadly poison. Hemlock is also a plant too poisonous to be used safely.

Each of the above can cause clear visions and make a person feel as if they're flying. However, there is a *very* small difference between an effective dose and a fatal one. Furthermore that margin would be narrowed or nonexistent for someone whose health was poor. It would also depend upon such factors as body weight, age and hormonal state. We don't any longer know how to take these herbs safely (if anyone ever did). Therefore, they should not ever be used. They should not be drunk, eaten, smoked, inhaled as incense or used in a massage oil by anyone. Our ancestors may have had some kind of knowledge of antidotes that made these herbs safer. Even so, I should imagine that there must have been fatalities and ruined lives.

The quest for a quick route into the world of visionary experience via drugs has always been popular – in spite of the risks. However, genuine hedge witches do not need to put their lives on the line nor risk paralysis each time they want to meet with the elves.

In common with most present-day witches, I advocate

the use of things like chanted spells, visualizations, dancing, spinning in a circle, or very safe herbal teas, such as eyebright or vervain, to open inner sight and promote spirit travel. These methods are slower for a beginner but with practice they will get you there safely and with all your wits intact. Indeed, I suspect that genuine hedge witches have always erred on the side of caution and simply got on with the magical work. Then as now, serious 'tripping' may have appealed to those who liked best to party but who were not naturally psychic. I am aware, in saying this, that indigenous shamanic traditions have often included a lot of imbibing of drugs that promote visionary experience. However, these practices were not hit and miss, with a random consumption of whatever herbs came the user's way. They were done in a disciplined and knowledgeable way.

The erotic route into altered consciousness is safe for us in the present day. It mainly consists of letting ourselves be immersed in the flow of dreamlike images that can arise during sex or after orgasm. There is actually no need for orgies, or bestiality or any other figment of medieval obsessional imagination. These visions can be explored in the context of any loving relationship. The method is dreamy, unstructured, experimental. At first, just watch the visions and enjoy them. Later, try being within the dreamscape. Look down at your envisioned feet. Are you wearing shoes? Is the ground stony? The sand of a beach? Grass? A wooden floor? Walk around and explore for a while, letting the dream unfold without effort.

Some present-day witches use wooden dildoes with ointments made from benign herbs in order to make this method more effective. I have not felt inclined to try this (or perhaps I am just not brave enough) so I am no expert on the recipes for these ointments. But I suggest using wheatgerm oil as a base in which to soak vervain,

mugwort and parsley for three days. After being strained
it is ready for use though it should be kept in a refrigera-
tor and then discarded after a few more days since it
contains no preservative.

If you find that this method works for you then you
could progress to ointment made with beeswax to which
you have added tincture of benzoin as a preservative (half
a teaspoon to each pint of ointment). Melt the beeswax
mixture and combine it with your oil mixture (the same
quantity of a vegetable oil as of beeswax). Such an ointment, if made with clean equipment and stored in a cool,
dark place, will last for weeks or months.

The above herbs are safe and gentle. Nevertheless,
mugwort and parsley should not be used if you are pregnant. And *any* herb may cause an allergic reaction so test
the mixture first on a small area of quite sensitive skin such
as your wrist.

Such mixtures are not only for the lone female witch. A
man can use them to anoint his penis – his very own
'broomstick'. Lovers can use the oil or ointment to
massage one another.

As you can see, the ways and means of working with
staffs and brooms (or their phallic symbolism) are many
and various. And the ubiquity of stick riding, or dancing
astride a staff as a means to induce spirit travel, shows that
it is a tried and tested magical practice throughout the
world, in a number of styles. This may be because so
many cultures have or have had the idea of a tree as a
cosmic axis, existing 'here, below and above' and therefore linking the different dimensions.

I do not incline to the Freudian view that an object with
a pronounced phallic shape, such as a tree trunk, must
always solely and forever symbolize a man's penis. In the
world of magical symbolism the other way round could be
equally true – that is, a penis could mean a tree. In any

case, in magical thought, images may be interpreted in many ways, and all are equally valid. That is, after all, what symbolism is for – to convey many themes and ideas in just one image. It is a way of using the mind that is fluid, poetic, inclusive, embracing of paradox, transcendent, wild.

Traditionally, many types of wood may be used for the making of staffs or brooms and these vary from land to land. In the Near East, according to Margaret Murray, witches flew on palm branches. Perhaps they still do. Scottish witches flew on something called a *bunwand* (a hollow stalk). The Siberian shaman had a birch pole as his 'spirit horse'. In Britain, the choice of steed has tended to be an ash branch or staff or else a broomstick with an ash handle. But the oak, birch, hazel and willow are also popular. In China, so far as I know, a giant peach tree was believed to be the cosmic axis. So perhaps Chinese witches fly on peach staffs or brooms.

There are other variations besides a choice of wood. German witches, like their British counterparts, ride on broomsticks. But they prefer to sit with the sweeping end forward, whereas in Britain it is traditional to have the bristles behind and the handle foremost.

In some shamanic traditions, the staff was tethered as though it were a horse that might wander off while the owner lay down in trance to get on with psychic work. This echoes Norse mythology, in which the World Tree itself transforms into the God Odin's horse, transporting him into spirit realms.

The hobby-horse, really a stick or staff with a model of a horse's head on one end, was ridden by shamanic practitioners in central Asia. A stick with a horse's head! This magical tool really does convey all that a witch means by broomstick riding: the World Tree as broom or staff as spirit horse for riding to other dimensions to speak with the elves. And, as we have seen, the World Tree and its representatives, the staff and broom, can connect us with spirit realms to rearrange the threads of fate as well – in other words, to cast a spell. A wand, as you may by now have guessed, is a pocket version of the staff. You can stand astride one, however small, and its use in spell-casting is too well known to need a comment of any kind.

In some cultures, the 'horse' or staff has been seen as an image of death. However, in riding one the witch did not court a physical death – or not unless those toxic hallucinogens were being used. Instead, the practice of entering trance was and is experienced as some kind of transformation that can be symbolized as a death or ending of everyday consciousness. It is not, of itself, any more life-threatening than going to sleep.

How would today's hedge witch go about broomstick or staff riding for spirit journeys? See the next chapter! But first, become properly equipped. You will need both a staff and a wand. The traditional way to get these items is as follows.

Obtaining a Staff or Wand

The best times at which to obtain a staff or wand are at a new or full moon or at a solstice or equinox or on any one of the four sacred festivals that fall between them (30 April, 1 August, 31 October and 1 February). The best times of day are dawn, noon or sunset. Obviously, if working in daylight you would ask the sun to bless with power. If working at night, the moon – unless it is a new moon when the power is strong in the daytime, the moon then being overhead although invisible in the bright sunshine.

Go to the tree of your choice, one that is of a species you believe to be right for the symbolic World Tree. Different tribes and cultures have had various ideas throughout time about which species this really is. North Europeans have seen it as birch, ash, oak, willow, yew or hazel. To some Native Americans it was or is the poplar tree. In India it is yew and in China, the peach. So, find a tree which feels right for you, for the purposes of your magic, even if it is none of those which I have mentioned here. Ask the tree, out loud or inside your mind, for permission to take some wood. If you sense that the answer is favourable you can proceed. If not, try another tree or try the same tree on another occasion.

Walk all around the tree till you see the piece that seems most right for your purposes, being about the right length and thickness for a wand or staff. The wood should be taken with a clean cut – and never just broken – so that the tree suffers minimum damage. Before taking the wood, say the following.

Old Lady, give me some of your wood
and I will give you some of mine
when I am dead.
And send your power into this branch
for the good of my magical work.

The above words are not mine; they are traditional and are addressed to the Pagan Goddess in her guise of wise woman/queen of the spirit reams and of the World Wood.

Then cut the branch, which should not fall to the ground when cut but should be held up. It is said to lose magical power if the wood touches the earth before being consecrated as staff or wand by you, the practitioner. That, at any rate, is the tradition. (Myself, I have not found that it makes any difference if the wood touches the ground at this point. So I wouldn't worry.)

Next, you should thank the tree, saying something like this.

Old Lady,
I thank you for the power
of natural magic within this wand/staff.
Let it remain powerful
for the good of all.

Place an offering at the foot of the tree. This should be ale or honey or bread or cake or three handfuls of a herb or seed. (Flax seeds are said to be most acceptable.) If the offering is a liquid one, pour it straight out upon the ground. If it is solid, sprinkle it just as it is with no plate or bag or other container and then lightly cover it over with some earth so that it is buried. Now consecrate the staff or wand, matching the following actions and words. Hold the staff or wand up to the light of sun or moon, then sprinkle it with salt water, then breathe upon it and finally visualize a strong, silver stream of light coming from its tip.

Sun/Moon, bless with power
and water with sacredness,
salt with safety,
air now inspire
and wraith now pattern
this wood to my desire!
I set it apart to do the work
of natural magic as a staff/wand
serving me well.
And in the names of the Lady and Lord
of elven realms within the World Wood,
I name it [. . .] and so cast the spell.
So may it be.

Here give your wand or staff its own name. This should be something that conveys the purpose. For example, you might call a wand 'Fate Weaver'. (It is traditional in Northern Europe to strengthen the magic in items such as staffs, swords or banners by giving names to them.) The staff or wand is now ready to use.

A staff or wand may be any length with which you are comfortable, but a traditional wand length is from your elbow to middle finger tip.

It is usual to strip your wand or staff of some or all of its bark and to remove any knobbly bits left over from twigs that were growing out of it. Obviously, you will want to do this after cutting it and before consecration. You may also want to embellish it by tying on bird feathers or carving runes or a pentacle or some other magical symbol into it. You need a long period of peace and quiet in which to concentrate on all this. Therefore, many people take the wand home to prepare it before performing the consecration.

To manage all this without putting your wand down is quite a feat – almost impossible in fact. Personally, as I said, I feel it makes not the slightest difference. I would quite happily use a wand that had touched the ground before consecration. I have often done so. I do not believe that the real magic is compromised in any way.

And that is just as well because, in common with many of today's witches, I sometimes pick up a fallen branch to make a wand or staff, rather than cutting one from a tree. Of course, I do not want any magical tools made from rotten wood so I always check that the branch is still sound and hasn't been lying there too long. This can be done by peeling back some of the bark. If the wood is still green underneath, it is quite fresh. If not, it may have been lying on wet ground for months and be rotten and brittle.

I would also use a wand or staff that had been gathered by someone else, provided I knew that they were responsible environmentally. Indeed, I do use such tools. It is said to be less effective, magically, because the wood has a connection with someone else – the one who gathered and worked on it, stripping the bark. This doesn't bother me as I always feel that the actual 'tree-ness', the natural spirit of a well-consecrated wand overrides anything else anyway.

A well-used wand or staff is said to become almost an extension of a natural magician, almost a part of them. Indeed, many magical practitioners were buried with their favourite staff in past ages because of this strong psychic bond.

Chapter 7

The Rite to Fly

Some of my favourite herbs for promoting psychic awareness and spirit flight are dandelion, eyebright, thyme,
vervain and willow. Other hedge witches may prefer bay,
dittany of Crete, cinnamon, lemongrass, mugwort or
yarrow. And there are many more possibilities from all
around the world. Such herbs can be drunk as a tea or
burned as incense, providing that you have checked for
medical contra-indications and general safety, especially in
the case of anything rare or unusual.

For the rite which I am about to describe and which is
designed to help you attain spirit flight, I recommend
vervain (*Verbena officinalis*) as this is gentle and as safe
as anything ever could be. It will increase your psychic
awareness and bring psychic protection at the same time.
For a stronger effect add mugwort (so long as you are not
pregnant) and thyme, which has long had a reputation for
helping people to see the faeries.

You can make tea out of these by pouring a half pint of
boiling water over the dried herbs in a teapot or mug. Use
two teaspoons of each herb. Let the tea stand for about
fifteen minutes and then strain it. The result will taste fairly
horrible so you may want to add lemon juice and honey to
make it a pleasant drink. Since the rite is quite a long one

you could keep it warm in a flask until you need it. The hedge witches of olden times, having no such thing as a flask, would have brewed it on the fire around which they worked or else drunk it cold.

I am not a fan of incense used outdoors. (Why go to a place with fresh clean wind, perhaps bearing the scent of wild flowers or salt sea or snow or the land itself, and add lots of smoke?) Indoors, you may want to burn bay, thyme or yarrow to cleanse the room psychically and boost your capacity for psychic experience. (Two magical effects from one incense – a bargain!)

On the other hand, if working outdoors in a garden or in, for example, a place where the wild thyme grows, you could inhale the scent of the fresh, living plants, for the same result – an increase of psychic awareness plus psychic cleansing.

The best time for a rite to achieve spirit flight would be at either the new or the full moon. That is because the new moon's magnetism and the full moon's light each have an effect on the human pineal gland, making psychic experience easier. (However, once you are experienced you can go spirit travelling at any time without such a boost.)

The best place would be any liminal area where you can be sure of freedom from interruption. (Therefore not the beach on a national holiday!) If you live in a crowded area it would be best to do this rite inside your home.

You will need a staff or broomstick, a wand, a bowl (made of pottery, glass, wood or any other organic material), some milk or cream and your herb tea (together with a chalice, mug or glass from which to drink it). Bring along also a notebook and pen in which to record your experiences. (As with dreams, it can become unclear exactly what happened unless you write it down.)

If you are dong this rite with a friend, another hedge witch, you will each need a staff or wand. You will also need to alter the words, substituting 'we' for 'I'.

The Rite to Fly

Begin your work with the first three spells in the 'Rite of the hedgerow', described in Chapter 4 (pages 60–4). That is, begin by standing in an actual or symbolic boundary and speaking your spell for communion with spirits.

Follow this up with the psychic purification spell. Now pass through the hedgerow or forest edge or other actual or symbolic boundary to your working area for the main body of this rite. If indoors, this will be in the most spacious area of the room so that you can move about freely. If outside, this will be a glade or a clear open space upon a hill or wherever you feel comfortable.

Finally, cast the spell to call upon elemental spirits for aid. If you feel the need for extra psychic protection during this rite, add the following words.

Spell for Strong Protection

I call to you, elemental spirits
within wind, light, rain, land and wraith,
to keep me safe by word and bell.
Keep watch and ward so all is well.
Turn away each harmful wight
that no bad spirit shall me afright,
in the names of the Mother and Father of all.

Now ring a bell. In imagination, project the sound into spirit realms. In many parts of the world, bells are used to attract friendly elves while at the same time banishing any hostile spirits in the vicinity. Ring it three times.

Lastly, invoke the Lady and Lord of the World Wood. You can use the words given in Chapter 4 (page 65) or some of your own.

Now make your statement about the purpose of this

rite. In Chapter 4, it was about helping trees. This time, you could simply say:

I am here to gain the blessing of spirit flight.

Next, you should call on the elves of that area.

Hail, friendly elves, here, below and above.
Hail and welcome!
Assist me by powers of beauty and truth and love.
Bless this rite of spirit flight.
I bring you these gifts.

Place your bowl on the ground or floor. Fill the bowl with honey, cream, milk, nuts, sweet cakes, fruit or any combination of these. (Later, the offering will be buried but it can stay where it is for the duration of the rite.) You should now also pour out your herb tea into your chalice, mug or glass.

Holding your wand, dance around in a ring, deosil (turning to the right). If space is limited, circle upon the spot. As you do this, hum a sequence of any three ascending notes (as in 'doh, ray, me'). Don't sing words but hum either 'la la la' or three *sounds* and hum them repetitively.

Feel the sound as though it wells up from the ground beneath your feet, rises through your body and comes out as you chant. Feel, in your imagination, as though you are humming the tune of the land. This is quite easy to do, actually. After all, we are not distinct from the Earth but aspects of her. Her minerals flow in our blood. Her elements, including her wraith, make us in body and soul.

You are raising the land's own magical, creative power within yourself. Let yourself sing about this. Words may come to you, spontaneously, when you have danced and hummed for a while. Alternatively, you can use the following incantation or part of it.

Spell for Magical Power from the Land

La la la, la la la
song of the land.
La la la, la la la
spell of the land.
La la la, la la la
power of the land.
La la la, la la la
power of elf-kin.
La la la, la la la
power from within.
La la la, la la la
power from the hill.
La la la, la la la
power of Earth's will.
Rise in me, rise in me,
rise in me, rise in me,
rise in me, rise in me,
rise in me, rise in me,
arise and fill,
fill me with power,
the power to bespell,
the power to bespell,
the power to bespell.

(The 'hill' in line twelve is a reference to faerie dwelling places which are sometimes known, traditionally, as the 'hollow hills'.)

When you have raised enough power – either by using this spell or another or just by dancing and humming – pour it straight into the herb potion via your wand. Mentally direct the power you have raised right into the liquid. Do this by using imagination to see the power of the land, that magical power, flowing along your arm and out through your hand

and wand as a stream of light. This is usually white in colour but it may be tinged with silver or green. Say:

I bless, consecrate and set apart this tea as a magical potion, by powers of wind, light, rain, land and wraith and in the names of the Lady and Lord of the land and of the entire World Wood, here, below and above. May it serve me well for magic uses as a flying potion, setting me free to travel in spirit realms, easily. Let it enable me to see and hear clearly the presence of elves, so long as this harms no one and does not transgress elven law or any courtesy. By this potion may I be changed, forever more, to a spirit traveller, a hedge rider. So may it be.

Drink the potion and also sprinkle some of it on to your staff or broom. When you are ready, take up your staff or broom and stand astride it. Say the following:

In the names of the Greenwood
Lady and Lord, let my spirit now fly.
Let me travel out.
Let me go to [. . .]

Here, name your destination. It may be whatever you choose. If this is your first journey, it would be useful to say, for example:

to meet with an elven friend, a familiar.

Conclude with these words, which are traditional:

Thout, tout a tout tout,
throughout and about.

Spin around on the spot or circle the room nine times, anti-clockwise, which is the direction magically linked with turning inwards to spirit realms.

The last two lines that you say ('thout, tout' etc.) are an old flying spell used by witches in Somerset in the seventeenth century. (I looked up the word 'tout' in the *Oxford English Dictionary* and it derives from the Old English 'totian' meaning 'to project, peep out'. So this spell is for spirit projection. In other words, for spirit consciousness to be projected from your body so that you can take a peep at the Otherworld or, if you choose, at a distant part of this one, independently of your body's actual physical location.)

Dismount from the broom and lie down comfortably.

You may now be wondering whether you must go through all this complex and lengthy ritual every time that you want to fly. Certainly not. The point of all this is to cast a spell enabling you to go spirit travelling in future. This requires developing the skill by constant practice. In order to practise, you need only do the following 'trance-meditation' or 'pathworking'. An experienced witch can travel anywhere, merely by lying down quietly and using a psychic technique such as the following. At that stage, you will not need any herbal potion or ritual nor an earthly broom.

Trance Procedure for Spirit Travelling

Wait until you are relaxed before you begin. If visions start to appear naturally and you find yourself wandering in a 'dreamscape' as a result of the earlier rite, just go with what's happening. You are already in some aspect of spirit realms. But if your wanderings lead nowhere definite and you are simply drifting to no purpose, pick up the thread of the following trance at the point when you look for a tree that seems, somehow, to call to you. If coming to this procedure without doing the earlier rite, start here – the rainbow visualization takes the place of the 'Rite to fly'. Visualize red light all around you. In the world behind your closed eyes (and they should be closed) everything is red. You are clothed in red and astride a red broom or staff, drifting gently downwards.

After a while, the light all around you becomes orange. Visualize it. Continue downwards upon a staff or broom that you now see as orange. See your orange hands grasping the handle. Everything is in shades of orange. (It doesn't matter if you don't see this clearly. Just do your best. The trick is to stop trying hard but to just do it in a relaxed way until the pictures begin to form of their own accord. At that point, you have left the constraints of your everyday mind and body and begun to travel.)

Then the light becomes yellow. You ride a yellow broom or staff downwards. You and the clothes you wear are entirely yellow.

Then the light becomes green . . . then blue . . . then indigo . . . then violet . . . You float down through each colour on your broom.

As you fly down from the seventh rainbow colour, you and your surroundings take on all the natural shades of a beautiful landscape – full spectrum light. Now leaves are green, the earth is brown, any flowers around you may be pink, white, yellow, purple, any colour. You are in a beautiful landscape and are beside a small grassy hill surrounded by forest.

Walk around the base of the hill in imagination. Go to where a track leads down through the woods to a river in the valley. Each side of the track are splendid strong trees, tended by land-elves who live in this place.

One of the trees seems especially beautiful or interesting to you. Look around in the woods till you notice it. This tree may be oak, ash, hawthorn, elder, goat willow, birch, crab apple or any type of tree from the land where you are living and in which you are now doing this spirit work.

123

Approach it. Placing one hand upon it, say something like this or with the same meaning:

By root and stem, leaf, fruit and flower
and in the names of the Lady and Lord of the elves
in their magical power,
I call to one in this place who will be my friend,
my trusted familiar. Hail and welcome.

Wait and see who now emerges, walking towards you from behind the tree or seeming suddenly to appear from out of nowhere. This may be a faerie creature such as a dog or bird (but it could be of any species) or an elven woman or man or simply a 'shape' of light, something abstract. In whatsoever form they appear, you will be able to speak with them, mind to mind. In faerie realms, language is no barrier. Elven beings can grasp our meaning, whatever our native tongue. Likewise, we can know what they communicate. It is beyond words but our own minds can usually supply words in instant translation. In this way, conversations are possible with elven (or earthly) trees and creatures as well as with people.

Introduce yourself and offer friendship. Explain to them that you are seeking the skills of magical healing so that you can help to heal trees and creatures, elves, people and places throughout the natural world. Explain any other aims you may have, such as learning how to restore the land's environmental harmony. Ask them if they would like to join with you in this work, giving help and guidance from faerie, while you undertake to *do* the spells in Middle Earth, physically.

If they agree to friendship, ask for their name. The first word that you hear inside your mind will be that by which you can call to them from now on. In fact, if the friendship proves successful, you will be able to call them, telepathically, at any time from anywhere, by using this name. Just repeat it, three times, inside your mind.

Ask them what they would like from you in return for their future help with your spells and their guidance in magical matters. (You cannot order real elves to do your bidding. Unlike the poor benighted house-elves in the Harry Potter novels by J. K. Rowling, real elves are free spirits in every way. They will be your familiar spirits only if they feel that you are as courteous as a friend should be. As we need to remember, the word 'familiar' actually means 'friend'. Any attempt to coerce an elf into being your helper will have only a short-term success at best.)

Your spirit friend may now ask you to follow them through the forest in order to show you what they will need from you or to instruct you in some form of magic.

Once, when I met my faerie teacher (a specific type of familiar of a very high order indeed) she took me back up through the trees to the faerie hill to show the answer. You may be taken somewhere quite different. If you are still having difficulty seeing anything clearly on your travels into the Otherworld, you can visualize what happened there to me – which I am about to describe – as though it were happening to you.

The more you practise visualization, the more you will develop the strength of your inner sight. Eventually, you will find that trees, elves, creatures, all kinds of beings are appearing to you of their own accord. For most of us, inner sight has been blurred by the lives we have led (full of stress and with an over-emphasis on what passes for rationality in the mainstream human world). Visualization helps to clear it.

If you are able to see your familiar or hear them speak with clarity, then follow their directions and see what happens next. If not, as I said, you can instead visualize the following as though it were happening to you. I shall describe it now in the present tense, as an extra aid to visualization.

I walk towards the faerie hill, following my elven familiar. We walk right into the hill on the west side, through a rock-lined passageway that leads to the hill's heart by a meandering route. In the hill's heart there is a huge, shining lake, glowing green and gold. This hill contains a whole country, or is a portal that leads to one. Its apparent size on the outside bears no relation to what is within. The water of the lake seems to reflect sunlight and trees, millions of green leaves, though nothing is up above except for the rock ceiling of a great cavern.

On the faerie teacher's instructions, I jump into the water. The lake is not what I expect. I fall right through it, as though through light and mist, gently drifting down. Below, I land on a seashore with many miles of glistening white sand. There, she is waiting for me and says that my blessing is what is wanted. She asks me to bless this entire faerie realm and all its inhabitants.

I turn around three times on the spot, deosil, then sink down on one knee, placing both my hands on the faerie ground. I say:

> I bless this land and all who dwell in it,
> May all be blessed, by three times three
> and in the names of the Lady and Lord
> of natural magic in all the worlds,
> with peace and good health and abundance.
> By wind, light, rain, land and wraith
> may this entire place and all who are of it
> be blessed with peace, health and abundance,
> blessed with peace, health and abundance,
> blessed with peace, health and abundance.
> So may it be.

I am then told to bestride my broom and fly up through the lake, above and through the earth and rock, to the crown of the hill. Passing through solid substances, like a ghost through a wall, I soon emerge. But I come out in the form of a tree or tree spirit. I have, by some mysterious alchemy, become one with my

broom and the kind of tree it came from. This has happened
without my willing it, quite naturally. I am tree, also human
and faerie – one with all – and I can see clearly the land's
powers.

Coiled all around the hill in glowing light is the shape of a
labyrinth. The tree that I have become stands right at its heart
on the top of the hill. The labyrinth is somehow <u>in</u> as well as <u>on</u>
the land. It is of the traditional type known as 'seven step' and
so is made up of two serpentine lines. These 'snakes' around the
tree are pulsing with energy. One of them is red, the other is
white.

I understand fram my faerie teacher, who has appeared along-side me, that these are Mother Earth's opposing forces including all pairs of opposites: expansion and contraction, summer and winter, giving and taking, intuition and rationality, gaining and losing, heat and cold, day and night, dark and light and even life and death. This does not mean there is one good snake and one bad one. Although they eternally struggle for supremacy (shown in mythology as two men who fight for the love of one woman, the Earth Goddess herself), they are each essential. Turn and turn about, each must have the upper hand for a while. This keeps all worlds in balance. It keeps all in existence. Each one in turn wins the heart of the Lady in her magic garden, the heart of creation.

These snakes, or twin 'brothers', are really one being, one Pagan god who has two aspects. These must achieve balance. And they always do. By alternating the victory, they stay at one in the faerie labyrinth and in all worlds, creating harmony.

At the centre of the labyrinth, we may meet either the 'monster', the opposing force, who wants to fight, or the object of love and desire, the one who presides in the magical garden. These wear differing faces according to who we are and how we perceive them.

I am a woman. I stand at the heart of the labyrinth at one with the Lady, the Earth Goddess whose daughter is queen of the elves. Yet I am aware that the serpentine opposing powers are also within me.

If I were a man, I might feel that I am both the traveller in the labyrinth and the snake. I win the heart of the Lady and so become one with her and with the garden. And this is so, whether I am the red snake or the white – and I can be either so long as it is in due season. Yet I am aware that the garden and also the Lady are within me.

I stand on the hilltop, a tree-faerie-person, at one with the serpents and with everything. This is an experience of ecstasy. For the moment, I am restored to health and knowledge. And when I travel back to the mundane world of Middle Earth, even though I shall not stay in this state I will have been changed by it. I will be stronger.

When I am ready, I walk out of the labyrinth by its coiled path. Then I bestride my broom and say, 'May I now return home. I give thanks to my faerie familiar for assistance and to the elven Lady and Lord of this place. Hail and farewell.'

Your adventures and insights in faerie may not have been at all like mine. But wherever you have been, you should now thank your elven familiars and the Lady and Lord of the elves, stand astride your staff or broom and say the flying spell ('Thout' etc., page 121).

Ascend the rainbow, flying gently up through each colour. Just above the red band of light, picture the room or outdoor place in which you are lying. Then open your eyes.

Record your journey and what happened to you in your notebook as soon as you can. This will help you to think about and to understand it. Even if, as a beginner, you feel that you didn't see much or go far, you may be surprised at how much there really was, once you start to describe it. Sudden insights or small glimpses are to be recorded and valued. They are your seeds of change.

If you are experienced or just naturally gifted, you may have been given advice on magic or given prophecies concerning the future. These should be written down to help you remember them.

Stand up and bestride your earthly, physical staff or broom. Circle or spin on the spot, nine times deosil. This will ritually return you to Middle Earth and the everyday world. There is no need to do this if you have just undertaken a spirit journey by the rainbow entry alone and without the 'Rite to fly' which here preceded it. However, if you have spun widdershins (anti-clockwise) at the start of your work, you should spin deosil at the end.

Not to do so leaves you, symbolically, still in faerie. It may seem nit-picking to bother about these small details but to forget them can bring bad luck – or so I am told. This is not because bad faeries are out to get us if they can but because it's like leaving a part of your soul in another country. This means you can't be entire and whole about your life where you are and disharmony is then likely to come about.

I hope at this point, you are not feeling disappointed, having seen nothing. If you are someone for whom visualization seems quite impossible, do not despair. After lying down to begin your spirit travels, try telling yourself the story of the above entry into elven realms. Tell it as though it were happening to you. Begin, 'I float down through the rainbow on my staff/broom surrounded by red light.' Continue the sequence in your own words. When you meet the faerie teacher, say, 'She takes me into the faerie hill by a winding path. I see a great shining lake.' And so on.

Telling yourself such a story can be an initiatory experience. And as you relax into it, you may begin to add details which I didn't mention. You may change parts of the story or even change all of it, after a while. This, too, is a form of travelling. But don't actually *try* to do anything other than stick to the tale I have told. Trying too hard is counter-productive. It will make you too tense. Just playfully tell the tale. You can even bring in humour and send up parts of it. If, at first, you want to make it into a joke, then simply do that. The elves are keen on good manners but they also like mischief and humour. Doing Pagan magic is not like attending a church. After telling the story funnily, try it some other way. Supposing you made it dark and threatening? Try it like that if the idea appeals to you (but be sure that you give it a good and harmonious ending). Or tell it just as I have told it or as though to a young child or in any other way that occurs to you. You may even start to see visions while story-telling

– once you have given up on ever seeing them!

Telling yourself or somebody else such a story during a rite is a most powerful way of casting a spell for the changing of consciousness and for the restoration of harmony during a time of crisis or ill-health. You may or may not ever see your familiar spirits by using this method but it can certainly help you to hear them instead. Ask them to tell a story through you, offering yourself as a medium for this purpose.

By whatever method you choose, it is important to commune with spirit friends. Hedge witches have always been assisted by familiars. Contacting them is one important way to make the boundary between ourselves and the Otherworld a place of union.

Notes on the 'Rite to Fly'

Have your wand with you when spirit travelling. That is to say, a wand you see 'with your mind's eye': your spirit wand, not your physical one. If you feel threatened by or uneasy with any kind of spirit you meet, point your wand at it and say (in your mind), 'I command you to take your true form, in the names of the Lady and Lord of magical healing.'

If the being before you has bad intentions and is not a friend, it will now be revealed as ugly in some way or simply made of a substance like dark smoke. In your mind, still pointing your wand, you should then say this or something similar.

Banishing Spell

Begone, in the names of the Lady and Lord
to the realm below.

131

I call now upon the elves, in their names,
that you may be taken down
and your evil dispersed.
Now down you go.

I am telling you this so that you will know what to do if you have an encounter that is disturbing. However, it is unlikely that you will be troubled much. It is usually when we forget to invoke protection from the elemental spirits, the Lady and Lord or our familiars, that we are open to being pestered by bad faeries or other malicious spirits. It is very much more likely that the first spirit that you encounter will be a familiar who was waiting for you with goodwill and eagerness. (It is in the interests of the faerie realm to make links with those in the human community who care about Mother Earth and the good of us all.)

Some spirits may have been with you in a past life. After all, you may have practised magic, even hedge witchcraft, in former incarnations. A long-term familiar may have been waiting for you to begin spirit flight and notice them.

Never, never tell your familiar's real name to another person. If you do so, they may feel betrayed and leave you at once. That is because, in faerie, to know someone's true name is to have power over them – potentially. (Remember Rumpelstiltskin?)

And here is another word of warning. Beware of giving up your commonsense. Never do that and never surrender your own autonomy to any spirit whom you can see nor to any 'guiding voice'. You are in charge of your life and you are responsible for what you say and do. Any alleged familiar spirit who suggests that you do anything harmful to yourself or to anyone else should be dismissed. Keep the following rule in mind: *I make my own deci-*

sions. Then mischievous spirits will be unlikely to bother with trying to misguide you. In other words, deal with spirit guidance just as you would the advice of your human friends. Listen respectfully but only act on it if you can see that – at the least – no harm is likely to come of doing so.

However, remember that vows or promises made in front of or to the elves must always be kept. Elves are sticklers for honesty. Very bad luck is said to come of breaking a promise or a vow in which they have been involved, even as witnesses. Think very carefully before you promise anything and try to write it down afterwards lest you forget it.

As I have said, such spirit flights as the kind I recommend arise partly from your imagination. They start there, but they can end in mystery. From them, people are sometimes able to return with new and true insights on magic, accurate prophecies and new creative inspiration. Imagination, though the world treats it with some contempt, is our launching pad for *real* spirit flight. Or, to put it another way, it can be our portal into genuine psychic experience within the Otherworld. This results in a merging of the elven dimension with our own, which greatly improves the health and harmony of all the natural world, or so the elves tell me. This merging is done, in however small and partial a way, each time that we make spirit journeys or, in some way, communicate with elves.

The witch on a broomstick, the hedge rider, can with elven help become someone who links the sundered dimensions of nature, connecting faerie soul with body. Such an achievement can help to bring a great healing for all of us, in all the worlds. It is a psychic and magical healing but can have sound physical results in a reborn harmony for humankind and the rest of nature.

Labyrinths

Labyrinths, such as that which appeared to me on the spirit journey described above, are another kind of liminal space of interest to hedge witches and an ancient part of the Northern European hedge witch tradition. This may come as a surprise, since most of us associate them with the Cretan minotaur story from Southern Europe. Actually, labyrinths have been found as rock carvings or cut out in turf or constructed from stones in almost every land on Earth. But the place where the greatest number is found is Scandinavia. Some of these are as old as the Cretan one and experts feel it is unlikely that the building of labyrinths started in Crete.

In Britain, wise women have often used stone, slate or wooden models of labyrinths, small enough to be held in the hand, to enter an altered state suitable for magic or spirit flight. This is done by tracing the pattern of the labyrinth with a finger tip, in and out to the centre and back, many, many times, while chanting either a spell or the name of a goddess, such as Ertha, Freya, Rhiannon, Arianrhod or Creiddyled.

In Sweden, cunning men ran in and out to the centre of full-size labyrinths to prepare for magic. In Germany, labyrinths often had or have two entrances rather than one, so that two young men can race each other in to the centre, where stands a woman, representing the Earth Goddess in her young, virginal aspect. The winner of the race 'wins' the woman. Such games are folkloric remnants of ancient rites symbolizing the fight between summer and winter, expansion and contraction, and so on, for the hand of Mother Earth. This is a fight of course which neither can win permanently for both are needed to maintain life's balance.

Chapter 8

An Elf and an Ancestral Spirit

'If you really want to become a strong hedge witch', says my faerie teacher, 'you must understand that to ride a piece of the hedge right into elfland you have to be able to see life from other points of view than the human. You start this kind of thing by becoming one with a tree.'

'What do you mean by that?' I ask.

'Well, you *know*,' she says. 'You have learned to do it before and now must begin to do this to an even greater extent and more regularly.'

She then describes the psychic act of becoming one with a tree (which I outlined in Chapter 5). And she adds the following.

'You must let the tree's awareness prevail. You feel its fears of humanity and the terrible chainsaws. You sense its joy in the presence of elves who tend the forest. You understand its bid for the space, the ground, in which to thrive. You host the forest fungi, as it does. You dread some insects and welcome others. You feel the turning seasons as ebb and flow within your own being. . .

'Next, you can transcend even tree perspective and all tree feelings because the tree itself can do this, easily – any tree. You then commune with the soul of the forest directly and can contact any spirit of plant or elf or creature within it, in any realm. This is not so much psychic communication by telepathy as simple *knowing*. You know whatever you need to know to cast spells for healing of the environment or any single plant or creature at such times. It is very easy.

'To achieve this brings a complete transcendence of your own everyday mind's limitations. You become one – however fleetingly – with all creation by merging with a tree. This brings tremendous magical power but of a kind that can't be abused. At such times, you can work magic with ease and playfulness. You can do this by – for example – shape-shifting into a bird that sits in the tree. A magical bird whose song is so potent it can change fate and change it as you desire. You are now faerie-bird-tree-human – all of these and more than these, transcending them, because you have been prepared to *be in union*. Still using your imagination, as in all this sequence, you sing your healing song. In this state, you cannot cast any ruthless spell that serves your own ends alone. Having raised magical power by deep communion with a symbol or representative of the World Tree, you can then only do spells which serve everyone, such as for the health of the land or the healing of humanity's relationship with the rest of nature.

'That which we serve serves us,' she concludes cryptically.

'But some trees have a spiteful nature,' I argue. 'They are embittered. They seek their own survival or that of their species. They are not necessarily at one with all, according to folklore.'

'It doesn't matter,' she replies. 'This is a deep and

subtle magic. Any such tree will be healed of bitterness and limitation of purposes by your preparedness to become one with it. You do not come to this exchange as a beggar if your heart is clear of any wish to harm or possess the tree and its powers. Now do you understand?'

'I do. And if only I could always live and feel as you describe. But I lose it quickly among the conflicts and rough and tumble of everyday life. And I do need to cast spells for myself and for others and not only and always for all creation.'

'There are many, many ways for a hedge witch to live and to learn the arts of magic,' she replies. 'And many, many ways to cast a spell for yourself or for another as well as for us all. But if you have been able to merge with a tree and experience harmony, you know yourself to be part of one double-natured being whom you might call Lady-and-Lord or Goddess-and-God. One with all life. And you can reconnect with this harmony – by prayer or spirit journeying – drawing upon it for strength to renew your magical and psychic vitality. Often the harshness of the human world can deplete a witch's magical energy, draining it along with hope. But a hedge witch who can merge with a tree and so become one with the soul in all, that person can recover an inner strength.'

'I see. Thank you.'

'Now I will teach you a method that elves use for casting a spell for yourself or another *or* for the world: an all-purpose spell. It is simply a three-step way to make a potion.' She continues as follows.

Fill a cauldron or bowl with clear water from a spring. Not everyone can do that, I know. Many humans live in cities, far from a fresh source. But all can use the freshest and cleanest water available. If you should buy bottled water, let it be from a spring as near as possible to where you are. If you use water from a tap, take a bowl of it and then sing or hum a tune to the water as a gift, an offering. If you can't sing, then play some music that is both peaceful and beautiful in the room where you stand the water. This will restore its natural magic – which could have been badly damaged by chemical cleansing agents and other things that human beings add to their drinking water.

This water represents the realm below. It is a medium of the dark-elves, since it has risen from underground where it has flowed in streams or gathered in lakes in unlit caverns. Remember, the dark-elves are not only concerned with putrifying matter, the composting of what is corrupt or rotten, but also with renewal. Theirs is the realm underneath in which a seed sprouts. Their concern is the dark of the womb as well as the tomb. Their work brings rebirth. So the water in cup or cauldron can contain your new vision, your new intention, your spell's purpose, with their blessing.

Begin your spell-casting in your accustomed way, calling on elemental spirits and elves for help with your magic. You can do this as simply or as ceremoniously as you choose. Invoke the Lady and Lord of natural magic in the World Wood, they who are deities of the elves in all realms, in Middle Earth and below and above. Do this in whatever style feels natural at the time. You could say, 'Lady and Lord, bless and ward me now.' Or something much more elaborate but with the same meaning.

Place your hands round the bowl or cauldron. Say this.

Cauldron Spell for All Purposes

Water, water, crystal flow
bring power of magic up from below
from that deep realm where the dead go

which is under the land
in spirit ground.

By dark-elves' aid, I charge you to hold
the dream that I tell. Bear my design
and carry my spell. By three times three,
the power of nine.

Tap the cauldron or bowl of water nine times with your wand. Then raise it above your head so that, if you are working outside, the sunlight, moonlight or starlight can shine on the water. If you are in a building, place it next to a lit candle, symbolizing the sun, moon or starlight, according to the time of day. Then say the next part like this.

Light-elves, bestow
the power of light
to merge with the water
in a dream, bright
as any rainbow.
And let this dream,
by night and day
prevail, coming true
in every way.
Be it as I say.

Place the bowl upon the ground. Add appropriate herbs for your magic. These might be rose petals for a love spell, lavender for a cure for insomnia, beech leaves for powers as a writer, ash or mistletoe to resolve a conflict, rosemary to dispel illness – or any other herb suitable for your particular chosen purpose. Or you might use a mixture of herbs, three or nine of them blended together.

139

Next you should say the third part of the spell.

Land-elves, I call you
to bless this blend.
By wind, light, rain, land and wraith,
my spell to tend
as it harms no one,
in power without end.

Add:

Let my intention come to be.
With the words that I speak now over this potion,

I name my wish, making it a decree.

Now breathe into the water a spoken description of what you want. For example, you might say, 'May my health be restored. May I thrive in strength and be full of vitality.'

Whatever the object of your spell, from prosperity to Earth healing, build up the detail of your dream by describing it fully. Direct it into the potion upon your breath by speaking it out aloud. Conclude by stating, 'So may it be.'

Well, that is the 'All-purpose cauldron spell', described to me by my faerie teacher. What you do with the potion depends on its contents and the spell's purpose. Here, commonsense, safety and creativity are some of the important factors. If you are entirely certain the potion is non–toxic, you can heat it in a cauldron or pan, allow it to cool, then strain and drink it. This would be the obvious thing to do with, for example, a potion for health or for clairvoyance. If casting the spell with or for someone else, you could offer them the drink as well. But if there is any doubt at all about the safety of the herbs in the cauldron, then you have quite a few other options.

For example, if the toxicity is very slight, you might anoint yourself or the other person on wrists or brow with the enchanted brew. If the potion is meant to affect a place – for example, as psychic purification – then you would sprinkle it all around the perimeter (or in each corner, if indoors) and in the centre. If it is meant to heal a tree or a creature, you might sprinkle it upon them. You might also use it to anoint a talisman, such as a crystal which you mean to carry as a charm for prosperity. And you could sprinkle a potion on to staffs or wands or other working tools, to consecrate them. You could even pour it into a river, to heal the area though which the waters flow.

Do not attempt to store such potions. They contain no

preservative and must be used within a few days. Pour the residue into the ground as this will present it again to the land-elves in thanks for their help in manifesting your objective.

Nothing which is seriously toxic is worth using at all. Never, ever put any poisonous herbs into your cauldron. Avoid also those such as cuckoo pint (*Arum maculatum*) which can be an irritant to the skin.

However, herbs which are safe and soothing can be added to your bath water, in any number of spells for beauty, sexual attractiveness, health, psychic purification and so on. On such occasions, you might add to the water in the bath a potion which you have already enchanted. Or you might cast an informal spell by treating the bath itself as a huge cauldron in which you can immerse yourself while doing the magic.

Be inventive. Any new twist which you can put upon the old idea of 'herbs in a cauldron' could be effective. Creativity is the life blood of hedge witchcraft. And nowadays we don't all have the kind of home in which we can boil up herbs in a cauldron over a lovely open fire. We are more likely to have to make do with some kind of saucepan and a gas stove. But by using the kind of spell my faerie teacher recommended we can make very powerful magic involving herbs – an enchanted potion – in almost any circumstances. Real magic can always adapt to the spirit and customs of any era.

My next account of herbs in a cauldron (or a cup) and of hedge witchcraft features a sitter in the hedge whose style is earthier by far. Her name is Melie and she was a country wise woman living in the West of England back in the nineteenth century.

I have communicated with her by psychic means. I did this using a technique of regression to a former incarnation, commonly known as 'past-life recall'. This technique is described fully in my book *Lamp of the Goddess*. In fact, I believe that she was me – or rather that I was formerly Melie. But it does not matter to me whether this is objective fact or an imaginative idea. What does matter is that her ideas and methods and attitudes are inspiring. I find them so. They are also authentic. That is to say, her information is compatible with other people's accounts of traditional practices. Perhaps I have made her up. If so, I think that a worthwhile exercise.

Whatever the case, here is a true nineteenth-century voice (with a West Country accent). She is a speaker without self-consciousness and without any idea of New Age philosophies since she comes from a time well before Paganism was influenced by such things.

In the following dialogue, the first voice is that of my husband Ashley, who encouraged Melie to speak through me by asking her questions while I was in a light trance.

A Melie, where is that you do your magic? Where do you normally go to cast a spell?

M Sometimes, I'm on that flat bit of rock up near the hilltop, back of our house. It's out of the way of most folks round here, so I can be on my own. Then I turns into a owl and flies out of my body – so as to go and seek out what I needs.

A And what sort of things do you gain by doing that?

M I find out what bad faeries is causing a sickness or else what 'uman it is who's harmed a woman by some bad wishes. Them kind of things.

A Do the people in your village know you're a witch?

M I'm a wise woman and a good Christian! At least, I tells
   'em that. And I say all this magic is just old wives' tales
   but it comforts people. That keeps 'em quiet.

A What do you do to get ready for leaving your body and
   being an owl?

M I drinks a tea that brings on the power. 'Tis only
   celandine. My mother, she swore by hops. Grand-
   mother, she liked her vervain. If you can sense what
   the herb is that would make you fly, that's one sign
   you're one of us. 'Tis only common herbs we do use
   in my family. They won't make someone turn into a
   owl who isn't born to it. If you'm a straightfor'ard
   'uman, 't won't do no good if you drinks a whole
   bucketload!

A Surely, you don't just drink a herb tea? What do you
   do after that?

M I told you. I goes on that rock. Or sits between two
   poles, my staffs of ashen wood. That's for when I'm
   in my house. Outdoors, I holds on to two little twigs,
   one in each hand or I puts 'em each side of me. Or I
   sits in a hedge or in that line of trees just over our
   pasture.

A Then what else?

M I makes it all clear first. I sends the bad away. I waves
   my birch twig over my celandine tea and all around
   where I be.

A As a psychic purification.

M Is it? I sends the bad spirits away. 'Go home,' I says, 'Go down. Go away.'

A Then you sit down between two poles or twigs and drink your celandine tea? And your spirit turns into an owl, at once? Just like that?

M That's my witch shape, dost see? My mother, rest her soul, she was a gander. What's think o' that, then?

A I think it's – surprising. Why not a goose? Surely a male witch would be a gander?

M You'm a tight-laced 'un. Well, I goes out to fly round till I finds out what's wrong. Then I calls out to the Queen Owl to come along. Sometimes, she comes with a lot of owls, crowds of 'em. She tells I what to do. Sometimes, 'tis only some little thing. Bring back a bit of bread, bless it in Queen Owl's name, give it 'em afore their dinner. Other times, might be a herb to hold in their hand. Or make a medicine for 'em to drink, with a spell what I've said over it, three times. 'Tis sometimes one thing, sometimes another.

A Is all your magic done just like that?

M 'Course not. Other times, I crush up snail shells or sea shells and mix them with mud in a pot. I think of what wants gone – an illness, it may be – while I smashes 'em up. On top of the mixture, I draws a pattern of what I wants instead. Good health, it may be. After, I puts a picture of a spiral going sunwise for that. Or I puts a tree with six little branches all pointing up at sky. After, I puts a black cloth on it for a night, covers it, see? Just like a babby hid inside its mother. Next day, I turns it round nine times, sunwise. Then I pulls off the cover and lets the light shine on it. After, I leaves it be till I has what I want.

A Do you call on any more spirits besides Queen Owl? Do you work your magic with aid from the Goddesses and the Gods?

M There's the White Lady of the Woods. Her tree is the birch. And the Old Man. I mean him what carries a lantern.

A Who is he? Do you mean someone you know in your village, a cunning man, another human?

M (laughing) No, my dear, he ain't a human. He's from the other place, not from this world here. A king witch, he be. He looks out for us all. He has a little white dog with him trotting along. And there's good kind St Margaret. I hope you'm not saying I ain't a Christian?

A (ignoring this) How do you get enough power when casting your spells? How do you raise power?

M What is it you're meaning? I got enough power!

A Where does this power come from? What is it?

M It's in the things I do use, herbs and such, and in me. And I brings the light of the moon in my body. When 'tis full, I goes outdoors in moonlight. Then I stands still and makes myself thinner. Well, not thin, I makes my whole body see-through, just like fine linen. Or like a ghostie. I does that by only thinking it so. Then I draws moonlight right in me by breathing it in and by letting it shine all down through me. That does my magic good. That helps it waken. Beforetimes, I brings it up from the land down below. I does that in my mind and then it happens like drawing water up well in a bucket. What helps my magic comes up from the land like a ghostie mist. And down from moon in that light that rings like a bell chime on one note that don't stop. How do you get it then? I heard of one got the power by having her hands buried up to the wrists in sand down on the beach. The tide come up round her. After, she could take folks' pain away with them hands and give 'em good ease and peace. And there's a man round here says if the setting sun shines on his fore- head, he gets the Sight and can tell of the future. Folks does all sorts. Why are you asking me all of these ques- tions? You should ask your own self!

Well, that was Melie. The huge difference between her style and that taught to me by my faerie teacher does make a really important point. In hedge witchcraft, there is no dogma, no question of one true way. All is creative, experimental, in spite of our being so firmly rooted in nature's cycles and in alliances with nature spirits in ways which are very old indeed. Nor would a present-day hedge witch necessarily think as Melie thinks – or thought – about all our practices. For example, I no longer feel that to be a hedge witch you must be 'one of us', born to it, or else the herb teas for psychic power won't work and your spells will fall flat. This is obvious nonsense. Magic belongs to everyone, everywhere. It's an ability everyone has, like the ability to communicate. Even the deaf and dumb can manage sign language or body language. Even the autistic can convey meaning and feeling by *absence* of speech and by withdrawal. Communication belongs to us all and so does magic.

While it is certainly true that some are more gifted at magic (or communication or anything else) than others, anyone can make a start at learning it. Magic exists, like music or colour, and so, potentially, it exists for us all.

Few people still believe that spell-casting power or psychic awareness are only given to those in witch families. It's as ridiculous as thinking that you can't be a musician unless your parents were. So, in my present life, I have grown well past that old-fashioned attitude. However, in many ways, I love Melie's ideas. And I love her humorousness and the way she sees no need to analyse what she is nor to justify it. She simply *is*. As for her style, I find it inspiring.

If you do *not* like Melie's approach and do not really like my present-day style very much more then that is fine. Do things your own way – so long as it works and harms no one. We have plenty of scope for innovation as hedge witches. We reinvent ourselves endlessly. That is why hedge witchcraft has survived and will most probably always be part of life.

Melie may have been myself in a past life. Or she may be the spirit presence of another person, someone for whom I can act as a medium. Or she might be an aspect of my own psyche, something a psychotherapist might call a sub-personality. Whatever the case, I like her attitude.

One of the reasons she speaks with such assurance as a wise woman is that she is thoroughly rooted in her local traditions, folklore and, last but not least, environment. Melie knows the names of the trees and flowers in her vicinity as well as she knows the names of her family. They are the herbs in what we might call the cauldron of her locality.

She does not have to wonder what a hawthorn looks like nor how to tell an ash from an oak tree. If you asked her what was the colour of a male blackbird's beak, she'd think you were crazy. After all, in her view, everyone knows! In her day, all country people and most townsfolk too could identify all common plants and creatures quite easily.

Believe it or not, a lot of today's people, in Britain anyway, cannot tell yew from cypress nor cowslips from buttercups. They would be hard put to identify birch trees or mimic a crow's call or tell where the moss grows. Throughout the entire world, folk are becoming more alienated from nature each day. They are not taught about it as though it were part of mainstream culture, the real world. Therefore they don't know how to value it, except in limited ways.

In urban culture (which is prevalent everywhere in Britain nowadays, even deep in the country), the land is perceived as a 'resource'. The natural world is seen mainly as a place to grow crops or from which to extract minerals or in which to relax in 'leisure pursuits'. For those who do not spend much time outside cities, it may seem even vaguer than that. A kind of backdrop. Just scenery.

From a Pagan point of view, it's no wonder we live in times of spiritual as well as environmental crisis. After all, few can respond with wonder and joy at the magnitude and wild beauty of all creation if they've been taught that there's nothing beyond the city but 'undeveloped' or 'developed' resources. And nothing in it worth noticing but other humans and their activities.

One of the main tasks for any apprentice hedge witch is to learn how to name at least the most common plants and creatures in her or his own area. Just what are the trees in your local hedgerow or forest or in your garden or city park? And do you know which ones are native species and which are not? Near to where you live, is there a river or a canal? What grows along its banks? What creatures live there? If you don't know, it is quite easy to teach yourself, using pocket guides to identification. (If you are learning about trees, don't do it in the depths of winter as most trees are more easily told apart by their leaves, fruit or flowers than by their bark.)

When able to identify trees and flowers, we are in a much stronger position for casting spells out of doors, with living species as our plant allies. After all, if you decide to cast a spell which involves sitting under an elder tree or inhaling the scent of a wild rose, it certainly helps to know in advance where these are.

Even in cities, there are still tucked-away areas, such as the banks of streams, alongside which there may be willow, elder, hazel and many other trees and wildflowers, as well as wild creatures, such as foxes, badgers, toads, slow-worms and dragonflies.

Cunningham's Encyclopedia of Magical Herbs by Scott Cunningham is an invaluable guide to the magical use of various trees and flowers from many lands. *Herb Craft* by Susan Lavender and Anna Franklin is another such guide and one I recommend wholeheartedly. My own earlier book, *Spellcraft for Hedge Witches*, contains a list of many European trees and herbs and their magical uses.

These days, in this particular age, there can be something subtly magical in merely learning to name wild plants and creatures, to identify them. It means we acknowledge their particularity rather than relegating them to anonymous and, by implication, unvalued types and species called 'just a weed', or 'some animal'. It is true that naming and labelling things can be used destructively, as in the kind of botany where we give Latin names to the various parts (having dissected the specimen), ignoring the wholeness of the plant and its spirit and denying its individuality. It is also true that in faerietales, we gain power over things by naming them. But *not* to name something or someone even as a type is plain dismissive!

Naming our local plants and creatures can be an informal spell of recognition and reconnection with their importance, their vital part in the web of life. When you say, for example, 'Hail, elder tree, old lady, wise witch of the woods', you can come into a good relationship with that plant's individual spirit and with the magical powers of that species (which in the case of elder are healing and helping the witch to see faeries or to commune with the dead). And if you want to pick the flowers of elder for medical purposes (such as to make a tea for the treatment of a feverish cold) then it is obviously vital to identify them correctly!

Elder is quite a common plant in Britain. Yet it is still important to take only small quantities of the flowers or fruit and take them only when we need them. The holly tree, once seen everywhere, is an increasingly rare species. This is because so many of us have taken berried sprigs for our Christmas or Yule decorations. It goes to show that even the plants we take for granted must be conserved if we are not to lose them completely. As for the really threatened species, no hedge witch need ever pick them, or any part of them. After all, no spell we could cast by doing so is likely to be as useful as letting them be. We can always find a less threatened substitute to use in magic. For example, we could work with dew that has been collected from the leaves of a rare plant without damaging that species in any way.

We also need to know at what times of the year our local plants come into flower and when they bear fruit. At such times, a plant is said to be specially potent for magical purposes. This is not a simple matter of saying all plants bear flowers in the spring and fruit in autumn. Reality is more complex than that. Ivy, for instance, flowers from October to December and the berries do not become ripe till spring. (This provides bees with nectar late in the year. It also means there is food for the wild birds at the tag-end of winter.)

What about other local creatures? When do they breed? Do any hibernate? Which ones? And when do the birds migrate? Which birds? A hedge witch should know these things though, these days, many of us do not. Or not all of them.

Out on the Somerset moors near to where I live, flocks of up to six million starlings sometimes gather. They can be seen all flying together in co-ordination. It is spectacular. All those millions flying as densely as bees in a single swarm and never an accident. No collisions. They wheel and dip and turn in the sky in aerial formation. What a display! If six million aeroplanes were to fly in such a way, making such manoeuvres, we should be stunned. (And deafened.) The birds seem to do it easily. It is as though they have one mind or are so attuned to each other that any tiny movement by one brings a response from all others in perfect harmony.

Nature stages a good many awesome events if we know where and when to look. By timing our magic to harmonize with them or at least with nature's cycles or peaks (such as a full moon) we can align ourselves with the greatest power. We can make very powerful magic because we are linking our own wills with enormous and kindred powers. And they will be kindred if we have objectives that resonate with their own or with qualities they possess. For example, imagine casting a spell for peaceful co-operation within a group – or among all people – while starlings fly. Imagine working while they're performing their aerial ballet above you. If you should call upon starling spirits for assistance and upon elves of the land and sky, you could work with ease.

Arguably, the starling spirits do not care one way or the

other if humans co-operate with each other. But you would not need to ask them to care – merely to ask them to bring the pattern of co-operation into your magic in exchange for your own co-operation with wild birds and their needs. For example, you might offer to help keep the moors free from damaging development. Or offer to feed wild birds regularly. Or study starlings and find out what they, as a species, might specially need. Above all, you might *ask* the starling spirits what they require if they are to help you. (Remember, you should follow their instructions, no matter how seemingly bizarre, but *only if no possible harm can come from doing so*.) Hedge witches may work with psychic and symbolic reality – but they are not irresponsible lunatics.

When we work creatively in this way, the boundary between ourselves and the soul of nature becomes, indeed, a place of union. This means not only that our spells are effective but that an integration is made between the soul of the witch and the greater soul of nature herself. This helps to heal the rift between humankind and the natural world, the psychic alienation felt by so many and which is the reason for so much abuse of the environment.

If we can experience wild creatures and elves as our kin and the Earth as our Mother and do it without any senti-mentality, we can restore a wholeness to the human psyche on behalf of all. This is the subtle but vital work underlying hedge witchcraft whatever the spell's purpose. Early hedge sitters probably knew this so well that they took it for granted. In today's world it could hardly be more relevant or more necessary. It is a psychic work that can reverberate throughout all existence, an unending magic, a spell of communion to which we can each contribute.

Hedge witchcraft is not about mystification but it is

certainly involved with mystery. That is why this book does not offer any closed fixed system but rather themes and suggestions. Hedge witchcraft is not complicated. When it comes down to it, hedge witchcraft is built upon just one paradox: *any boundary is a place of union.* The ways to make magic out of this are many and various but it *is* the great law (or lore) of hedge sitters.

Any two opposing states are closest right at the barrier between them. Whether that boundary is the border between two countries or the skin between two lovers, it is the place where they can touch each other. Boundaries and borders are made to delineate and to keep things in or else to hold them out and are essential. But they are also places where we begin understanding of all that's beyond us. Therefore, they are places of deep transformation and so are magical.

By treating a hedgerow or other boundary as a symbolic barrier between humanity and the rest of nature, we can cast spells which help to heal the relationship between humanity and the rest of the natural world. By calling upon the elves, elementals and nature spirits for assistance, we can do this as a group effort, not merely by pitting our own small will against gigantic corporations. And if this does not always work out exactly as we might hope or expect, it is certainly not without any effect. There is one thing of which I am certain as a hedge witch and it is this. No healing spell is ever a waste of time, even if its results may be in some way surprising or happen less quickly than you expect.

Melie might have been surprised to hear that her magical work could be perceived as having a profound healing effect on the world, something which went way beyond each separate spell's purpose. But I, her spiritual descendant and possibly her reincarnation, am living in a world which is rediscovering ideas that had been lost in the nineteenth century. These, however, would have been known to the wise of an earlier era when Pagan spirituality held sway. I do not imagine they would have been understood by everyone. But by a good many *hagazissas*, priestesses and priests, shamanic practitioners and others, I think they would. That which is undertaken on a deep psychic level affects us all, for good or ill, because our minds and souls and spirits as well as our bodies are a part of the greater life of all creation. In Pagan thought this is understood.

Chapter 9

Walking with Elves

A perennial tradition such as hedge witchcraft must have been a fluid and adaptable thing throughout all the centuries, always able to be reinvented in keeping with each fresh era. It has to be like that now, as well, in order to survive. Nothing which *lives* is static and unchanging. Therefore, we must be sometimes experimental with our magic. Serious though our purposes are, it is a bad idea to be always long-faced, grave, formal. Experimental approaches are often playful.

And if we cannot laugh at ourselves or take a fresh, even a quite silly step, we can lose touch with the elves. It is well known that the faerie realms are often full of laughter and that the fae love jokes and tricks.

Ideally, we should take magic seriously but not ourselves. Then our best spells will be more powerful because they won't be undermined by a self-consciousness born of pomposity. This more relaxed approach allows us to improvise, casting a spell suddenly, at need, without any pre-planning. It sets us free to 'walk with the elves', hearing their voices and seeing them sometimes more easily because we've become free of expectations.

Bearing these ideas in mind one day, Ashley and I

decided to do magic without an entirely structured plan. We would use no more than the opening and closing sequences to a hedgerow rite and a simple welcoming of any elves who came near us to watch or to work magic. We wanted to do something that was both simple and playful – and then see what happened next. We wanted communion with the elves and their assistance in our environmental magic but not to plan it all.

It is very helpful to practise hedge witchcraft with knowledge and discipline. This gives us confidence and it ensures that we reach a point when we can dispense with formality and yet find that we have enough skill to play at magic with style and get real results. This is quite different to playing at witchcraft if you don't really know what you're doing. *Then* you may cast spells irresponsibly or else just ineffectually. The witch who has basic competence can find that being playful enhances the magic.

Accordingly, Ashley and I travelled one summer day to Cerne Abbas in Dorset, to do a rite with a playful element and a loose structure. We had decided to go through a hedge backwards. We thought this would bring slight disorientation which would undoubtedly help us in reaching an altered state. The idea came because we'd been joking about the old saying our mothers used when we'd been out playing as children and came home untidy: 'You look as if you've been dragged through a hedge backwards!' We said that they must have known we'd grow up to be hedge witches, often appearing with leaves and twigs sticking to us when we'd been out spell-casting. Also, we knew that there were old Pagan healing rites that involved pulling somebody through a cleft in a tree or a blackberry thicket, the idea being to leave behind illness or evil spirits on the other side. We didn't know if they went through backwards though.

We did our work on Giant's Hill which is just outside

Cerne Abbas village. As you may know, the hill is named because of a huge man carved in the chalk there. This drawing is visible for miles and consists of a naked man with an erection, holding a club. No one knows how old this figure really is. Some estimates say about fifteen hundred years and some much less. In any case, the image in folklore and for Pagans today depicts the God of nature at his most fertile. However, we were not there that day to do any kind of fertility rite but had chosen the site because it holds magic of many kinds and because it has comparatively wild country in close proximity to a human community (the village of Cerne Abbas). Thus, we could work with the old technique of walking from a human settlement into a quieter, wilder place for the purpose of linking human reality with that of elves and nature spirits by treating the walk as a magic rite.

In common with most Pagans, we believe that the chalk giant is there because the hill has always been sacred, and *not* that the hill is sacred because of the drawing. We also believe that fertility may mean magical creativity – and many another kind of abundance – as well as the conceiving of children. And I'd like to emphasize that the rite that follows did not have to be done there or anywhere with similar associations. We went there because we like it and live quite nearby. The hill is surrounded by unspoiled, partially wooded hills and valleys for many miles. Undoubtedly, the beauty of such a place is helpful to magic.

At the start of the rite, we stood in a hedgerow at the bottom of Giant's Hill, but facing backwards. That is to say, we faced away from the direction in which we now meant to go. We had come from the village and meant next to go uphill through the woods to the wild, wide plateau up on the ridge. But we faced the village. This meant that we had to start by saying:

We stand here upon a boundary.
Before us, there is a human community.
Behind us, the realm of the elves
in the natural world.

(Normally, of course, it would have been said the other
way round.)

We continued our rite with the 'Spell for communion
with wild spirits' and then the 'Spell for psychic purification', followed by the call to elemental spirits and then
'Invocation of the deities'. (All of this was as described in
Chapter 4, pages 60–6.) We then said something like
this.

May we be blessed with elven guidance
from our familiars and elven help
with our spells for the land.
Here we stand upon the boundary
between the elven domain and humanity,
both here and there.
Let us go backwards to find now
an ancient harmony with the elves -
a world of peace and co-operation
in playfulness and creativity, bright and fair.

Then we went through the hedge backwards. We had to
turn round again and walk forwards in order to go through
the woods to the top of the hill. This was because the
terrain was too rough for us to be able to walk it without
seeing where we were going (too many tree roots, too
many badger holes). At the top, we were able to go backwards under a hawthorn arch for the last few yards. Then
we were in a grassy sunlit area swept by a warm breeze.
The entire wide hilltop stretched out before us. Beyond it
were other hills in the mellow light. The pale flowers of

chalk downland in an English summer were all around us looking as though they were straight from faerie, being ethereal yet bright. We poured out spring water and milk upon the ground and placed honey at the foot of a tree on a plate of leaves. All these were offerings. Then we said this. Or words that meant this.

We welcome you, friendly elves here in Middle Earth. We welcome you who tend nature's balance, the health of the plants, places and creatures. Land-elves of this place, dark-elves below, light-elves above, all you who come and go hereabouts, creating harmony by joy and laughter, magic and bravery. Hail and welcome! We bring these offerings. We ask your blessing upon our magical powers. We ask for guidance in casting spells to help and heal the natural world. We ask you to blend your magic with ours. As we walk in this place, we ask you – be with us.

Then we set off on a walk on the top of Giant's Hill and along the adjoining ridge. On the way, I saw an elven woman whose body was made of that light that used to be called 'royal blue' (electric blue). She was in a small grove of birch and hazel trees and as she watched us walk past she raised one hand as though in blessing and then – she vanished.

When we had found a sheltered place not too near the path, we sat down to speak with the elves – mind to mind, as in telepathy. We communicated with our familiars and also with those elves who lived in the vicinity (in the more subtle dimension of the land-elves). By now, our psychic senses were wide awake.

I was given the following guidance by my faerie teacher that day. It concerned the reasons for disharmony between humanity and the natural world *and* advice about a particular spell I could cast to help do something about that disharmony.

'Humanity', she said, 'does need to become free from the many spirits of abuse and exploitation which are possessing the souls of many people. These spirits have often actually been *created* by human beings and they have run rampant.

'I am using the word "spirit" in a broad sense here,' she continued. 'It includes all manner of psychic entities, including those which you call "bad thought forms" or else just "bad energy fields". By whatever names we know such things, they perpetuate abusive culture throughout the world. They are the spirits of greedy, destructive using *patterns* of behaviour which exist on the psychic level and influence people's physical actions. They incline people to take what they want without caring who or what suffers. This means there is much exploitation of plants and animals and places as well as of other human beings.

'These abusive spirits and their psychic patterns are, for the most part, the result of humanity's uncaring behaviour which is caused, in its turn, by lack of spiritual evolution. Therefore, time will bring a remedy since human beings will grow into wisdom and a sense of responsibility – when the time is right. Meanwhile, these ghouls are making things worse because they are part of a vicious circle in which they help to create the behaviour which creates them and so on and on.

'But fortunately', she said, 'there exists a psychic equivalent of the land's ability to make compost out of things that have become rotten. (And that is what these bad spirit patterns really are. They're the instinct for life and survival and comfort and plenty turned to corruption.) That equivalent, as you know, is the realm of the dark-elves. In that land, all psychic material is purified and may be transformed to become psychic nourishment for new growth. It is "composted" or baked or compressed or broken down, as in alchemy.

'So the patterns and entities of abuse of the natural world must be sent down to the realm below to be transmuted. This must be done without any harm to anyone. It is not only immoral to curse particular individuals or corporations for harming nature. It is also *useless*. That is because the bad spirits which are possessing them will only fly to another person and so the harm goes on – even if bad individuals actually die. All the while that abusive spirits are wandering in the world, there will always be someone to act as a host for them. And so the harm goes on.

'The only real answer', she said, 'is for magical healers of every kind – the hedge witches, shamanic practitioners, Wiccans, Druids, priestesses and priests of every culture – to join with the elves in banishing all abusive spirits from Middle Earth, as best they can. Send them all down below to become psychic compost. Many people are doing this work in their own creative ways, without knowing they do so. In fact, every time that someone refuses the opportunity to abuse or exploit something and then uses their frustrated desire to fuel the search for a kindlier option, they have joined with the dark-elves to achieve transmutation. But a magical practitioner may do this work consciously – on behalf of humanity as well as for themselves.'

I was then instructed to go and ask a blackthorn tree for the gift of three of its fruits (sloes) to use in my spell for the banishment of some ghouls. And afterwards, I went back down to the hedge at the base of the hill and then walked through it as a ritual act of returning to human territory – Middle Earth. There, I had been told to say a spell and after that to cast on the ground the three sloes. (Any part of the blackthorn tree is especially potent for spells of exorcism or banishing.) This was the spell – so far as I can remember. At any rate, it was something like this. The words used at the time came spontaneously or were spoken through me by my faerie teacher.

Now may all spirits of human abuse
of the natural world around here be banished
into the realm below.
There may they be withered, dispersed, composted
as any rotten flesh eaten by worm or crow.
May they become the psychic energy
nourishing co-operation and peace
between humanity and all species,
between humanity and the land.
Now by the magical powers of the dark-elves
and by wraith, land, rain, light and wind
and by the blackthorn and all her kin
and in the names of the Lady and Lord
of natural magic in the World Wood,
so may this be – so long as it harms no one
and serves all nature's good.

With the last words, I cast the sloes on the ground at the edge of the village.

I really must emphasize here that the spell was in no way a curse aimed at any human nor at any part of the 'human spirit' as a collective thing. Instead, it was directed at what I call 'bad spirits of abuse'. These are, in fact, ghouls (for the most part). They are strong emanations of psychic energy (created by humans) which survive in Earth's psychic dimension, influencing events and actions in just the same way that a bad psychic atmosphere in a house can incline its inhabitants to hostility, violent impulses, self-destructiveness and depression. The village of Cerne Abbas is certainly not a favourite gathering place for such entities. But they are everywhere. Some may be found around almost any human community, drifting until they find some human being prepared to let them have influence.

My spell may have dealt with only a few of them. It

would be asking rather a lot that one act of magic – even with elven help – should clear the whole of that part of Dorset. (We hedge witches are not quite so grandiose!) But it is better to do just a small amount of this work than to do none at all because we can't do it all. As I have said, the land needs more of us, more people to do this kind of healing – and other kinds as well. Meanwhile, I do what I can.

Ashley, who had stayed up on the hill, came down a bit later on and made for the village's holy well. He had been instructed by the elves to do a spell for the increase of woodland throughout the land – a spell for more green places, using water.

Then, together, we concluded our rite in the usual way, thanking the elves, the elemental spirits and the Lady and Lord. After which, we went straight to the Royal Oak for beer and some food.

That was an unstructured rite which began with a playful act (going through the hedge backwards) and became serious. It felt to me like a great success. Other hedge witches have their own style and might not have felt at all comfortable with a procedure like that. There is room for us all and each must find their own kind of creativity with hedge magic.

It is also important to experiment until we find the approach that suits our own era as well as ourselves. Hedge witchcraft as it was practised three thousand years ago in Germany or five hundred years ago in England may not be appropriate today. Different times require new approaches – a different aesthetic and understanding. It *is* important to find out – in so far as we can – what our ancestors actually did with the themes and ideas common to hedge witchcraft. But times move on and there is such a thing as evolution.

As I have said before, we are not a historical recon-struction society but *today's* magical practitioners. We should always respect tradition and base our work on received ideas *but* be creative and experimental. Any perennial tradition must always have been rather like that or would have died of its failure to grow and change and adapt.

For this reason, no apprentice hedge witch will use my spells and rites forever. After all, they are just one way in which this magic can be practised. Next year, I myself may be doing things differently. But, dear reader, please absorb the themes and images from my spells. *They* are tradi-tional. They are the spirit. The words and style of working are mainly my own. But the skills of natural magic which I have described and the practice of walking between worlds, sitting on boundaries, speaking with elves, these things are eternal and part of a heritage. Do with them as you will but hold them sacred.

As you become more experienced, you will begin to use your own words or to work silently (if that suits your nature). You will have begun to find the boundary between this great tradition and your own culture in whatever spir-itual, social or ethnic way you interpret that word. As always, you'll find it a place of union and therefore fertile. And this is good. Myself, I cannot imagine how anyone could ever want to walk a magical path that isn't exploratory. . .

The Wheel of the Year

Many may wonder how we can experiment with hedge witchcraft while celebrating the Wheel of the Year – the eight Pagan festivals so popular with witches. Here are some of my current ideas. (You may have others.)

Imbolg (1 February) The Hedge of Light

This festival is known as 'The first stirrings of the light'. It is a time of purification and inspiration because the daylight begins just a little bit earlier than it did at mid-winter. So we feel renewed.

If working indoors, make a symbolic hedge of flame to cerebrate the light. Outdoors, look for a hedge bearing early blossom, as does the blackthorn in a mild winter. Or work in an especially bare and bleak hedgerow that lets the light through. Do spells of psychic cleansing for your-self or for others. And spells to bring new inspiration and will to humanity to live in harmony with one another and all the natural world.

Spring Equinox (21 March) The Hedge of Nests

A time of renewed fertility and new growth in the natural world. Images and themes of this festival are eggs and hares (or 'Easter bunnies') as symbols of fecundity.

Work indoors with symbolic nests made of woven twigs or other materials and with hand-decorated eggs covered with images of anything we want to see increased, such as trees or any threatened species.

Work outdoors in a hedgerow or forest edge where there is nest-building.

A good time for spells of renewed balance between humanity and other species. And for all spells of increase and abundance.

Beltane (30 April/1 May) The Hedge of Blossom

This festival celebrates wild places and wild, unauthorized love. Traditional Pagan rites take place in the Greenwood and can involve love-making with a human partner – or a deep communion with an elf. The interface is between cultivation and the wildwood, rules and passion, humans and elves, or between lovers.

Work indoors surrounded by flowers and house plants or outdoors in a thickly blossoming hedge or deep in the forest.

A good time for spells to promote a greater awareness of and love for natural beauty and all wild places. In fact, a good time for any spell for love or beauty or greater freedom.

Summer Solstice (21 June) The Hedge of Green

A time of maximum greenery (in the northern hemisphere) as well as of maximum light. All trees and hedgerows flourishing with green leaves. This festival is the time of fulfilment – or that is its Pagan association. A time of the heart's desire, whatever that may be for any one of us (and not of consumerist substitutes). Therefore a time to celebrate or invoke for genuine happiness. Also a time to banish whatever distracts or obstructs anyone's fulfilment of healthy longings. (Imagine that! A world where most beings of all species were usually fulfilled. It seems to me there would be far less violence, far less trashing of nature and less greed. Less of anything born of bitterness, deprivation or fear of being unloved.)

Celebrate indoors, beginning between two staffs decorated with green leaves. Enchant a drink (such as rose petal wine) as a potion for happiness. Drink it yourself or – preferably – share it with a friend or lover. Sprinkle some drops on the ground as a spell for happiness for us all.

Celebrate outdoors in a hedge or forest edge at your favourite place or around any beautiful garden. Do the same kind of spell as indoors but hold the potion up to be blessed by the sun.

In Southern Europe, the sun was traditionally seen as a

Goddess called Sul or Sulis or Sunna. There are also sun Gods, such as Balder or Bel, in Northern Europe. And there are light-elves connected with solar light.

<u>Lughnasadh (1 August) The Hedge of First Fruits</u>
This festival celebrates the first signs of the year's harvest. It is also a traditional time to make any sacrifices that may ensure a better result (in any area of life). For example, a hedge witch might now make a vow to give a regular donation to a charity for tree preservation. Or to give up smoking for the sake of good health.

Work indoors with an altar resplendent with produce from fields or gardens surrounded by hedgerows or with hedgerow fruits. Work outdoors in a hedgerow or forest edge with the first fruits appearing. (There may be early blackberries and some wild strawberries.)

A good time for spells to bring social justice to ensure everyone gets enough to eat. Also for spells to promote fair trade and organic farming. (May harvests be great! May prosperity increase for all such as these!) In fact, a good time for 'last chance' spells of increase for anything. (Last chance in that particular year.) Pots of jam, loaves of bread or hedgerow fruit salads may be good mediums for your enchantments. For example, bespell some straw-berry jam as a potion for good fortune – to be shared with your 'community' (your family or friends) invited to a small harvest tea.

Autumn Equinox (21 September) The Hedge of Riches

Within the agricultural year, this is the traditional time to calculate the profits and losses. (Now that the harvest is gathered in, how well did we do? How much did we lose? And what do we learn from all of this?) It is also a time of simple thanksgiving. The same themes can be applied to any area of life.

Work indoors with bowls full of good food to represent what there is of gain and bowls full of rotten blackberries; or mouldy bread to represent what is wrong – in your own life or in the human community's relationship with nature. Give thanks for the first and compost the second.

Work outdoors in a hedgerow laden with fruits or an orchard or fruitful wood (where the hazelnuts may be start-ing to appear). Do much the same kind of magic. Or work with a labyrinth, constructing one from string or stones as a spell for land healing.

Samhain (31 October) The Hedge of Shades

In Northern European tradition, this is the time of the year we remember the dead. In mainstream culture, the day has degenerated into the mock-gothic excesses of Hallowe'en. But it is the best night in all the year for communing with loved ones who have passed on to the 'Summerlands' (the Pagan paradise).

Work indoors by candlelight among leafless twigs. Or outdoors at a place where a hedge or woodland edge used to be but has since been cut down or by a tree stump. At such places we can sense the ghostly hedge or spirit forest of what used to be – and can cast spells for the rebirth of such as these.

Yule (21–23 December) The Evergreen Hedge

Yule is the time of maximum darkness, though it is now that the light is 'reborn'. The folk tradition in Britain includes the making of wreaths at this time, from holly, ivy and other evergreen plants. These circular decorations, made to be hung on doors or placed on tables, represent the truth that the circle of life is always unbroken, even at the very darkest times.

Work indoors with evergreen plants or outdoors in a hedge containing holly, ivy, box or yew – or any ever-green. Or by a green tree. These plants keep the thread of green life when all else is leafless. It is easy to see how their magic could be woven into spells for the environ-ment and the sustaining of the biosphere at this time of enormous threat.

Indoors or out, hang sparkly objects, such as ornaments of coloured glass, to cast spells for the light of awareness to dawn on humanity – about what we should all do to live in harmony with the natural world.

Natural magic is always most powerful when worked at times of maximum psychic and magical power within nature, such as full moons, new moons and the eight festi-vals just described. For hedge witches, any day's dusk or dawn are also especially important as these are liminal times. They are both boundaries and 'thresholds' between the day and night. In their half-light, elves are said to be much more likely to walk the Earth. Thus, we can much more easily meet with them.

The hedge witch has always worked upon (or walked across) boundaries between our everyday world and the elven realms. So she or he is very well placed to make that long-awaited quantum leap on behalf of humanity. The one in which we *understand* our oneness with all aspects of creation. This can be achieved through communion with faerie spirits and those of trees, creatures and the entire World Wood. At this point, we truly experience ourselves as individual expressions of one great being – our Mother Earth. We know we are not apart from but a part of her, along with all others in all Earth's dimensions. In view of humanity's increasing alienation from nature, this is important.

Never were hedge witches more needed nor, in a sense, more privileged.

With such an awareness of interconnectedness, oneness, interdependence with all beings in all dimensions, humanity could not continue to pillage and damage and pollute the Earth. Our human ways would become very different. We would live lightly upon the Earth in greater joy and increasing wisdom. This would stem from a true sense of kinship with one another and with all species in all the worlds. It's a tall order for most of humanity – who are struggling to survive wars, diseases, hunger or various types of religious or political or social tyranny – to achieve such a mystical state. But the hedge witch (along with many, many other kinds of magical and spiritual practitioners worldwide) can do so on behalf of her or his community. That was our role, always: to do our 'spirit work' and achieve states of psychic communion on behalf of the tribe in which we lived.

Inherent in our spell-casting and our rites is this: the *possibility* of transcending – spiritually – all boundaries that separate people from one another and from the elves and nature spirits. We may not all achieve it each time that we cast a spell. Some of us may rarely do so at all. In any case, the experience may not mean that we live ideal lives and are always at peace with everybody. (I wish!) But each time that we work magically in a liminal place we may manage (if only for a brief time) to make of a boundary a symbolic place of union between all spirits. And each time it happens, it brings about a great deal of healing in all the realms. Or so the elves tell me.

Perhaps this is what hedge witchcraft was for, back at the innocent dawn of time. It certainly went down hill afterwards. Like every other human system of spiritual, magical, religious or psychic practice, it fell prey to various kinds of abuse. But what I have been taught by the elves – and have described in this book – is a very long way from a bid for magical power for power's sake. And a very, very long way from using magic to acquire other people's money or for revenge.

Time moves on – or moves in a spiral. And there is actually such a thing as evolution in magical practice and in human culture and understanding. Sometimes there *is* a great leap forward.

Addresses

Association of Hedge Witches
www.sothisstar.co.uk

The Woodland Trust
(*a charity that protects Britain's ancient trees*)
Autumn Park
Dysart Road
Grantham
Lincolnshire NG31 6LL
www.woodlandtrust.org.uk

Greenpeace
Canonbury Villas
London N1 2PN
www.greenpeace.org.uk

Wildlife Trusts
National Office
The Kiln
Waterside, Mather Rd
Newark
Notts NG24 1WT
www.wildlifetrust.org.uk

Rae's Website
www.raebeth.com

Bibliography

Anderson, William, *Green Man: The Archetype of our Oneness with the Earth* (HarperCollins, 1990)

Bates, Brian, *The Real Middle Earth* (Pan Macmillan, 2003)

Beth, Rae, *Hedge Witch: A Guide to Solitary Witchcraft* (Robert Hale, 1990)

—*Lamp of the Goddess* (Robert Hale, 1994)

—*The Hedge Witch's Way: Magical Spirituality for the Lone Spellcaster* (Robert Hale, 2001)

—*Spellcraft for Hedge Witches: A Guide to Healing our Lives* (Robert Hale, 2004)

—*The Nine Magical Ways: A Guide to Enchantment* (an ebook from Hexenpress, available at www.raebeth.com)

Bloom, William, *Working with Angels, Fairies and Nature Spirits* (Piatkus, 1998)

Conway, D.J., *The Ancient Art of Faery Magic* (Capall Bann, 2004)

Cunningham, Scott, *Cunningham's Encyclopedia of Magical Herbs* (Llewellyn, 1985)

Evans-Wentz, W.Y., *The Fairy Faith in Celtic Countries* (Dufour Editions, 1992)

Franklin, Anna, *The Illustrated Encyclopaedia of Fairies* (Vega, 2002)

—*Familiars* (Capall Bann, 1997)

Fries, Jan, *Helrunar* (Mandrake of Oxford, 1993)

—*Seidways* (Mandrake of Oxford, 1996)

Froud, Brian, and Berk, Ari, *The Runes of Elfland* (Pavilion Books, 2003)

Harrison, Michael, *The Roots of Witchcraft* (Frederick Muller, 1973)

Higginbotham, Joyce and River, *Pagan Spirituality: A Guide to Personal Transformation* (Llewellyn, 2006)

Howard, Michael, *Mysteries of the Runes* (Capall Bann, 1994)

Knight, Peter, *Thirteen Moons* (Stone Seeker, 2007)

Lavender, Susan, and Franklin, Anna, *Herb Craft: A Guide to the Shamanic and Ritual Use of Herbs* (Capall Bann, 1996)

Macdonald, Gillian, and Penberth, Jessica, *West Country Witchcraft* (Green Magic, 2007)

Murray, Margaret, *The God of the Witches* (Background Books, 1931)

Mynne, Hugh, *The Faerie Way* (Llewellyn, 1996)

Pennick, Nigel, *Practical Magic in the Northern Tradition)* (Thoth, 1989)

—*Mazes and Labyrinths* (Robert Hale, 1990)

—*Secrets of East Anglian Magic* (Capall Bann, 2004)

Romani, Rosa, *Green Spirituality* (Green Magic, 2004)

Roney-Dougal, Serena, *The Faery Faith: An Integration of Science with Spirit* (Green Magic, 2002)

Runic John, *The Book of Seidr* (Capall Bann, 2004)

Sjoo, Monica, *The Norse Goddess* (Meyn Mamvro, 2000)

Starhawk, *Webs of Power: Notes from the Global Uprising* (New Society Publishers, 2002)

Stewart, R.J., *The Well of Light: From Faery Healing to Earth Healing* (Muse Press, 2004)